The Whirlpool that Produced China

SUNY series in Chinese Philosophy and Culture
———————
Roger T. Ames, editor

The Whirlpool that Produced China

Stag Hunting on the Central Plain

Zhao Tingyang 趙汀陽

Translated by

Edmund Ryden

SUNY
PRESS

Cover: Stag Hunt. Attributed to Huang Zongdao (active ca. 1120). Handscroll; ink and color on paper. Metropolitan Museum of Art. Edward Elliott Family Collection, Purchase, The Dillon Fund Gift, 1982.

Published by State University of New York Press, Albany

惠此中国: 作为一个神性概念的中国

The translation and publication of this book was made possible with the generous support of the Berggruen Institute.

Berggruen
Institute
Ideas for a changing world

Printed in the United States of America

For information, contact State University of New York Press, Albany, NY
www.sunypress.edu

Library of Congress Cataloging-in-Publication Data

Names: Zhao, Tingyang, author | Ryden, Edmund, translator
Title: The whirlpool that produced China
Description: Albany : State University of New York Press [2024] | Series: SUNY series in Chinese Philosophy and Culture | Includes bibliographical references and index.
Identifiers: ISBN 9781438498966 (hardcover : alk. paper) | ISBN 9781438498980 (ebook) | ISBN 9781438498973 (pbk. : alk. paper)
Further information is available at the Library of Congress.

Contents

Foreword

ROGER T. AMES

With the precipitous rise of China over the span of just one generation, we are in our historical moment experiencing the effects of a dramatic and accelerating reconfiguration of economic and political power in the world. The Chinese ascent has certainly ushered in a sea change in the geopolitical order, but how will this new tide in the economic and political configuration challenge the prevailing cultural order that has long been dominated by a powerful liberalism? What impact will Chinese ecological values—a philosophical tradition that begins from family rather than individuals, from the primacy of vital relationality rather than the integrity of discrete entities—have on the evolving world culture in our immediate moment and the ensuing decades? And how will these values again reverberate within the ongoing, ineluctable transformation of the geopolitical order?

The idea of *tianxia* 天下—conventionally translated as "All under Heaven"—is a familiar term in everyday Chinese parlance that simply means "the world." But *tianxia* is also a geopolitical term found throughout the ancient canonical literature that has a deeper historical and philosophical meaning. Over the past few decades, the significance of this technical term as a possible Chinese framework for thinking about a new and evolving world order and a new model of world governance—sometimes referred to as the "All under Heaven System" (*tianxiatixi* 天下体系)—has, primarily in the Chinese literature, been a subject of much debate. Although the understandings of *tianxia* are many, within the Chinese process cosmology, this idea begins from an ecological understanding of international relations that acknowledges the mutuality and interdependence of all economic and political activity. *Tianxia* as "the world" assumes the primacy of vital relationality, thus relegating the nation-state as a discrete, sovereign entity to the status of a second-order abstraction from the vital, organic relations that constitute it.

Where did China as *tianxia* come from? Over the past few decades this is a question that has absorbed the thoughts of many of China's best historians and now, in this monograph, has been engaged by the contemporary philosopher Zhao Tingyang 趙汀陽. Zhao, keenly aware of the persistent and pernicious asymmetry in the prevailing way we have gone about theorizing China according to Western concepts and categories, has tasked both Chinese and Western scholars alike to "rethink China" (*chongsi Zhongguo* 重思中國).[1] To this end, Zhao introduces what he terms a distinctively Chinese centripetal "whirlpool" model of world order to interpret the historical progression of the *tianxia* identity construction on the Central Plain of China.

This process of identity formation has been driven by a series of interrelated "cultural attractors," with perhaps the most significant among them being the Chinese written character, but also including the canonical texts that perpetuate a shared cultural identity, and the political theology that emerges from this core culture. These attractors have drawn disparate populations on the Central Plain of China and its surrounding territories into a vortex, a whirlpool that was already taking shape more than three thousand years ago during the Xia, Shang, and Zhou dynasties, and that then continues in protean form down to the fall of the Qing dynasty. In this book, Zhao is forwarding a novel and compelling thesis on not only how we should understand China, but also until recently, how China has understood itself.

In this succinct yet ample work, Zhao, as one of China's most distinguished and respected intellectuals, provides a profoundly original philosophical interpretation of China's story. While in the spiritual world of China, its history and its canonical texts are drawn together as one, these classics and China's evolving history have set the standards against which each of them has been measured. In his efforts to interpret China's historicity philosophically, Zhao touches on many questions in many relevant areas of knowledge, from the discovery of the oracle bone script and China's exciting century of archaeology in which the ancient silk and bamboo manuscripts are continuing to be recovered, to the theorizing of China's history of thought and its sociology, politics, and economics.

Speaking of the realities of today, this continent called China is at once a state, a civilization, and a history. But in its temporality, the China that is a state, the China that is a civilization, and the China that is a history did not all happen simultaneously. Rather, these Chinas have happened in staggered stages that, in the end, have merged together to produce a vital and generative unity. What then, asks Zhao, are the causes, the forces, and the destiny that have coalesced to produce the one rich conception of China as state, as civilization, and as history?

In this monograph, *The Whirlpool that Produced China: Stag Hunting on the Central Plain*, Zhao sets out to give a philosophical interpretation of China's historicity. This book explains how the expansion of China was not due merely to the interchange among the disparate civilizations, nor to the lures of expansionist behavior in the form of military conquest, but rather to the fusion of the distinctive contributions of the many contenders for political control as they were constantly being pulled into the swirls and eddies of the whirlpool. It argues that drawn into this whirlpool of growth and amalgamation, the peoples surrounding the plains on all four sides sought to win the greatest material benefits and greatest spiritual resources by shaping their ways of thinking and living around the evolving core spiritual culture of the Central Plain. This book also investigates how the *tianxia* vision of world order was able to transform the fierce currents of contention within the whirlpool among the many cultures and many peoples with many ways of life and forms of governance and, for long intervals down to our present day, to draw out of them a unifying current.

Zhao explains the reasons why China became China by weaving together ontology with a game theory methodology. A fundamental issue engaged by Zhao is how the ontology of "becoming" and the vital eddies within the whirlpool became the methodology of China's evolution. And the primary question this book seeks to answer is how this core culture of the Central Plain became a virtually irresistible attraction to its vital periphery to the extent that, once a population and territory was drawn into the whirlpool game, it was difficult if not impossible to withdraw. In thus interpreting the structure of China's historicity, Zhao invites the past to become present again and to thus engage with the contemporaneity of the present time. In this way, an understanding of the contemporaneity of the past foreshadows the contemporaneity of the present.

Zhao Tingyang is a philosopher. In asking the question "Whence China?," he begins from an ontological answer that he draws from the first among the Chinese philosophical classics, the *Yijing* or *Book of Changes*. The fundamental reason for existence itself is the unceasing process of procreation, of generation and regeneration (*shengshengbuyi* 生生不已). As the *Book of Changes* announces, "The greatest capacity of the cosmos is the production of life itself" (*tiandizhidadeyuesheng* 天地之大德曰生). Zhao appeals to the archaeological scholarship of Xu Hong, whose notion of the "earliest China" (*zuizao de Zhongguo* 最早的中国) can serve as a point of reference to establish the tentative trajectory of a universalizing, all-inclusive, and distinctively Chinese generative process of geopolitical order called *tianxia* 天下. The erstwhile beginnings and evolution of this conception of world order reaches back into the mists of history before the Xia, Shang, and Zhou dynasties to what prominent archaeologist Su Bingqi has called a "sky full of constellations" (*mantianxingdou* 满天星斗)—a description of the many different, independent, and unique civilizations, each with its own narrative integrity, that were spread out across the central Chinese plain and the four surrounding areas. In this earliest period, *tianxia* references an emerging, holistic world politics that, as an inside without an outside, is at once diverse without being fragmented by the notion of determinate and bounded nation-states. Cosmologically, and religiously too as a natural theology, *tianxia* is a process that in its evolution establishes a cultural center for the earth and, in so doing, sets an axis that sanctifies the human world in its veneration of *tian* and the earth.

Importantly, Zhao's question is not "What is China?," which would suggest the search for some necessary, essential, and defining element to circumscribe this geographical and political entity. China in its original formulation is *tianxia*, an unbounded process of growth in world order. For Zhao, China is not a place, but a "taking place"—a world-making out of a centripetal whirlpool that over time has taken the mere "variety" of the constellations of many different cultures and, on the basis of their vital, ecological interdependence, has transformed them into a shared syncretic "diversity" in which the differences that obtain among the many different peoples are activated to make a difference for each other. Zhao, in reflecting on the emergence of this shared cultural and spiritual identity called China, dismisses the anachronistic language of the modern, particularly Western academy—terms such as nation-state, nationalism, dynastic succession, and imperialism. Instead, he follows earlier philosophers such as Li Zehou in asserting the intimate relationship in the most ancient times between shamanism, political leadership, and the historical record that has led to the continuing historical awareness and spirituality integral to the evolving Chinese *tianxia*.

Zhao selects his own metaphors. For Zhao, the economic and political motivational structure for the growth and continuity of China can best be described as a lengthy, continuous game—a "stag hunt" (*zhulu* 逐鹿) for political power—in which the issues, purposes, and very nature of the game are determined by the collective behavior of historical actors making rational choices directed at maximizing their interests. In selecting this game metaphor, Zhao is alluding to a passage in Sima Qian's *Records of the Grand Historian* that observes, "The Qin empire having lost its stag, all of *tianxia* were on the hunt for it."[2] The game achieves its "focal point" or historical order from the most advantageous choices of the collective of players and ultimately becomes their common history.

Zhao's second key metaphor is the centripetal whirlpool with its various cultural attractors exuding an irresistible force that draws the disparate populations into a game from which they neither want nor are able to extricate themselves. Certainly favorable terrain, climatic conditions, convenience in transportation, a concentration of wealth, and other material factors that usually conduce to civilization among human populations were an inspiration for would-be competitors to join the game. But Zhao argues it is the spiritual attractors that were the most powerful force in bringing together *tianxia* as an emerging political and cultural union out of difference.

First among these resources were the written Chinese characters, a development that wrested a monopoly on history owned by the political leaders through their shamanistic practices and made a shared historical narrative available as a unifying human resource. The written characters served as a sophisticated system for perpetuating a cultural corpus that, standing independent of the many spoken languages of the various peoples drawn in by it, could be read by all of them. At the Museum of Writing in Anyang in the middle of this same Central Plain, we see on display today a vast collection of the oracle bones that constitute the earliest extant record of this writing system. Remarkably, this sophisticated Shang dynasty script already in its own time had a vocabulary of over five thousand characters, a number that exceeds the normal literacy of an educated Chinese person today.

Zhao argues that this writing system was a technology of enchantment, a kind of magic, that enabled human beings to grasp the past and anticipate the future, and in so doing, transform time into their own self-awareness, self-narration, and historicity. This system established a legitimizing spiritual world the ownership of which gave political leaders the narration of an authorized history and the capacity for knowledge production that could be used to organize the hearts and minds of the people. The written language was the powerful medium through which norms, laws, and institutions could be established, interpreted, perpetuated, and employed, and it thus carried with it a determinative force that far exceeded economic influence and military prowess. Galvanizing the spiritual importance of this writing system itself was what it was used to convey: the shared narration of history and the values of a common lineage. The cultural corpus perpetuated through the compilation of the canonical texts provided a growing population with an evolving, collective spiritual identity and the development of a common cosmology through which the human experience could be organized and explained. Indeed, within this spiritual world, these classics and history were aspectually one, reinforcing and lending authority to each other. And even while, during different historical epochs, the center of the whirlpool would shift geographically from north to south and east to west, the continuing spiritual center was this culture of the Central Plain.

One significant element in this worldview was the *tianxia* system with its mandate of *tian* (*tianming* 天命) developed by the Zhou dynasty that, being an unbounded and inclusive conception of world order, invited all players regardless of status or pedigree to take part in and compete for the control of the economic and political order. What it did too was to afford the winner of the stag hunt for *tianxia* with legitimacy by locating the current dynasty within a continuing natural and political theology, a single, exclusive lineage that dates back as far as the remotest traces of a continuing, glorious history. It was a history in which all believed, and to which all deferred in practice through a ritual social grammar and a regimen of seasonal sacrifices to the ancestors. Again, this political theology was for any hegemon playing the game rationally justifiable as the strategy with the lowest cost for legitimizing his claim, while at the same time paying the highest economic, political, and spiritual dividends.

It is not until the Qin and Han dynasties that this earlier understanding of *tianxia* is revised with the establishment of China as a state within this all-inclusive world order. In thinking through what terminology best describes this new Chinese entity—empire, civilization, civilization-state, nation-state—Zhao makes the important point that its internal structure is a microcosm of the unbounded and inclusive notion of *tianxia* that had preceded it historically, and that it thus retains *tianxia* as its philosophical outlook. The gene of the original *tianxia* with its values of "being a match with heaven" (*peitian* 配天), "no beyond" (*wuwai* 無外), and "compatibility" (*xiehe* 協和) was the alternative to any kind of nationalism, a much later phenomenon that only emerged at the end of the Qing dynasty when a beleaguered China was set upon by imperialist powers that sought to dismember and consume it.

When we reflect on Zhao's compelling account of Whence China?, it provides us with insight into how to revise our understanding of the basic terminologies through which the story of this continuing Chinese narrative is told. We might begin by citing distinguished British sinologist Angus Graham, who would claim that different cultures produce different conceptual structures that best expresses their most important and enduring values: "That people of another culture are somehow thinking in other categories is a familiar idea, almost a commonplace, but one very difficult to pin down as a topic for fruitful discussion."[3]

How then, stimulated by Zhao's account of *tianxia*, can we rethink the language we use to understand and explain China? If Zhao's account of *tianxia* prompts us to think of China as the *dao* 道 or "way-making"—the central axis of a continuing and generative cultural lineage—we can discern how the political theology of such a cultural identity is "the weaving together of many threads" or the evolving confluence of many *daos* across the millennia: the *dao* of Fu Xi and Shen Nong, of the Yellow Emperor, of Yao and Shun, of Wen and Wu, of Confucius and Mencius, of Dong Zhongshu, and so on, down to our own time and place. Importantly, these *daos* are not confined to some retrospectively determined orthodoxy but include all of the different populations and cultures that have been drawn into the whirlpool. And just as this postulate is helpful in explaining continuity, it also works the other way in emphasizing multiplicity. For example, *tianxia* as a centrifugal vortex provides a way of thinking about the constant and continuing cycle of consolidation and diremption that has been the dynamic calculus of China's narrative. It provides a vivid image of the ingesting spire of centripetal consolidation that defined the swelling centers of the great Han and Tang dynasties, and its descent into the excreting, centrifugal gyre in which the many were disgorged from the one during periods of interregnum such as the Nanbeichao and southern Song. It is during these many times of disunity that the question "How do we determine which one is China?" becomes a point of deliberation. It also explains the hydraulics of the whirlpool when during the Yuan and again the Qing dynasties the Mongols and Manchus join the stag hunt for *tianxia* as initially "foreign" usurpers only in the fullness of time to become Chinese themselves. And in this process of identity formation, they swell the girth of a relatively stable center radially, to include the outlying territories within the orbit of the *tianxia* domain.

Another familiar Confucian expression that can be better understood by Zhao's account of the *tianxia* process is *he'erbutong* 和而不同, often translated into English as "the pursuit of harmony rather than sameness" and occasionally understood negatively as a dialectics of assimilation. But such a translation and interpretation does not do justice to Zhao's understanding of the *tianxia* game, where rational choice among historical actors is the pursuit of maximum benefit at minimum cost. This sense of purpose suggests that *he* is better understood as an optimizing symbiosis—the unrelenting and assiduous effort to maximize the creative possibilities of difference to animate the intergenerational transmission of an always emergent cultural identity and shared political theology. There is an understanding of cultural identity that appeals to the creative "doings" that are the distinguishing feature of humankind, and to possibilities rather than necessity. That is, rather than being guided teleologically by some divine hand or transcendent purpose, culture is understood as a contrapuntal responsiveness between human beings and their world to elaborate upon it, to elevate it, and through this collaboration, to achieve a decidedly aesthetic, spiritual product. As such, the pursuit of such superlative harmony does much of the work of teleology as a determining factor in the flourishing and consummation of the human experience. This optimizing harmony, resourcing the historical past as its reservoir for analogy and projection, draws upon human resolve and imagination to forge an always new way forward. The human capacity for design, purpose, and direction assumed in this Confucian sense of harmony gives the human being a vital and prominent role in the evolution of an emergent and always provisional social, political, and ultimately cosmic order.

When we reflect upon the story of China, the cultural narrative is truly a distinctive one in the human experience that is related through these key philosophical concepts. There is an intergenerational continuity captured in a term such as *ru* 儒, not understood as some potted and exclusive "Confucian" ideology, but as that continuing social stratum—the multivalent literati class of each succeeding generation—that is responsible for the inheritance, embodiment, and perpetuation of the high culture that is always evolving and made different in every age. And this continuity is also expressed as *xiao* 孝, the primary moral imperative and value system of the tradition that in the Chinese character itself combines "elders" (*lao* 老) and "offspring" (*zi* 子). *Xiao* reflects the assumption that the progenitors of each generation quite literally live on in their progeny, most obviously physically, but also culturally and spiritually. The persistence and tenacity of this Chinese cultural continuity stands in stark contrast when compared with ancient Greece and that contemporary political entity called by the same name, where any assertion of a continuing Greek cultural identity is rather thin by comparison. And the same can be said in important degree of ancient Egypt and that country today, or ancient Persia and Iran, or ancient Rome and today's Italy. Unlike the fading in time of these other remarkable ancient cultures, the *tianxia* game has had its tenacity and resilience where the past is very much present in the contemporary world.

The New Confucian philosopher Tang Junyi like Zhao Tingyang draws upon the cosmology of the *Book of Changes* in characterizing this continuing cultural process with the protean expression, *yiduobufenguan* 一多不分观, that we might translate as "one is many, many one." This persistent feature of *Book of Changes* cosmology provides us with another language for conceiving of the generative *tianxia* model of identity formation. Tang would insist that this postulate is a distinctive and generic feature of the processual cosmology locating the evolving formation of particular cultural identities as vital and specific foci that have implicated within them a boundless field of relations. Tang's ecological postulate insists on the radical contextualism and embeddedness that is ontologically defining of all vital things within their process of becoming. Importantly, *yiduobufen* is another way of describing the doctrine of intrinsic, constitutive relationality that stands in stark contrast to a concept of external relations obtaining among discrete and independent things—the ontological distinction between "becoming" and "being" that Zhao Tingyang explores in earnest. *Yiduobufen* is, simply put, the assumption that in the synergistic compositing of any "one," there "becomes" implicated within it the contextualizing, unbounded "many." And further, that in this process of transformative syncretism (*hua* 化), as the one changes the many, so the many change the one.

This *yiduobufen* proposition can be read in many different ways, as it speaks at once to the inseparability of the one and the many, to the continuity between particular identity and context, to the co-presence of uniqueness and multivalence, to the mutuality of continuity and multiplicity, to the inclusiveness of integrity and integration, to the dynamics of a shared harmony emerging out of relational tensions, to the expression of the specific details in the totality of the effect, and so on.[4] If we use the achievement of cultural identity as an example, it also restates in a different language the focus-field conception of cultures, where each culture, and each impulse in the life of each culture, has implicated within it the boundless "many" of its surrounds.

Like *tianxia*, far from being a pattern of many being assimilated into the one, Tang Junyi's *yiduobufen* postulate asserts that identity formation in this *Book of Changes* process cosmology is effected collaboratively within the cultural ecology. What Tang means by this claim is that if we begin our reflection on the emergence of cosmic order from *tianxia* and the wholeness and inclusiveness of lived experience, we can view this experience in terms of both its dynamic continuities and its manifold multiplicity, as both a ceaseless processual flow and as distinctive, consummatory events. This postulate is one more example of the mutual implication of binaries that characterizes all phenomena in the natural world—in this case, particularity and the totality, self and other. All unique events or foci are constituted by an unbounded field of more or less relevant relations that collaborate together to sponsor them, and they achieve their individuated identities as a function of the quality of coalescence they are able to achieve within these unique fields of relations. That is, moving from description to prescription, a dynamic reading of *tianxia* as *yiduobufen* is a summary of the way in which the opportunity is available to each entity to optimize the possibilities that honeycomb the relationships between it and its environing conditions. Not only does any phenomenon or event have implicated within it the contextualizing, unbounded many, but further as a unique "one" it is shaping and being shaped, and can find resolution and be focused in many different ways according to the multiplicity of perspectives that come to be defining of its evolving narrative. Importantly, any claim to its uniqueness and individuality, far from excluding its relations with other entities, is a function of the quality that it has been able to achieve within the unique configuration of these same relations.

Zhao's whirlpool model of understanding China as an inclusive *tianxia* certainly stimulates us to rethink some of the key philosophical vocabulary that can be drawn from the Chinese canonical texts to understand this evolving cultural tradition. But perhaps in addition, it can have broader application in providing us with a different way of understanding the changing geopolitical configurations of our own times—and anticipating their future possibilities. For example, how can the "stag hunt" for *tianxia* be deployed to illuminate the complex histories and emergent identities of immigrant nations such as Australia, Canada, and the "United" States, with their own versions of cultural hypergoods? How can this whirlpool model and its cultural attractors be invoked to help us understand the now fraught but still noble vision of a European Union, a Europe that in our own time is struggling to transform itself, with its own persistent and disintegrative Westphalian assumptions, into a *tianxia* model of economic, political, and cultural order "with European characteristics"?

More immediately, we recall that at the end of 2013, China introduced what it calls the "One Belt, One Road Initiative" (BRI) (*yidaiyiluchangyi* 一带一路倡议). From the Chinese perspective, this bold initiative is touted as nothing less than an evolving program of collaboration that, with its vision of "*intra-*" rather than "*inter*national" relations, will transform the existing world order from top to bottom and in all of its parts. Rhetorically there are two espoused values that ground this rhetoric of BRI, "equity" (*gongying* 共赢) and "diversity" interpreted through the language of a "shared future for the human community" (*renleimingyungongtongti* 人类命运共同体). Perhaps Zhao's notion of *tianxia* provides an alternative explanation to the uncritical Western assumption that China's ambitious strategy for effecting an alternative world order is a contemporary iteration of the West's own imperialistic history. *Tianxia* provides an ecological model of IR that begins from an acknowledgment of interdependence in all political and economic activity, and that advocates for hybridity rather than assimilation. As with the *yiduobufen* syncretism, "transformation" (*hua*) means that just as the one changes the many, so the many change the one.

China, in its unwavering commitment to proceed with this geopolitical strategy for an unprecedented scale of world economic development, if sympathetically understood in terms of its own history and identity, might be parlaying *tianxia* into a new world politics. Such a reading of *tianxia*, if laid out clearly by the Chinese academy as the interpretive context for BRI, might have the positive benefit, both domestically and internationally, of setting in a concrete way the appropriate aspirational targets for this initiative, and of providing a basis for evaluating its successes and failures. A standard can be established for assaying and defending the successes of BRI and, at the same time, for recognizing and thus minimizing its failures. Zhao Tingyang's notion of *tianxia* as a way of articulating and promoting the values of a cultural and spiritual China drawn from its own canonical texts can be used to exhort the economic and the political Chinas, to live up to their own rhetoric, and to thus lead the way into a more equitable world order.

Preface

This book tries to give a philosophical interpretation of China's histo-ricity. The spiritual world of China combines history and the classics in one. The classics and history set standards for each other. Outside history there are no classics to speak of; outside the classics there is no history to be related. Therefore, to use the methodology of philosophy to think about what China is, it is necessary to touch on many questions in many relevant areas of knowledge: the history of thought, sociology, politics, economics, archaeology, oracle bone scripts, ancient documents, and ethnology. In these areas, I have benefited from help given by many scholars, including Li Zehou, Qiu Xigui, Huang Ping, Zhang Yuyan, Yang Nianqun, Xu Hong, Zhang Wenjiang, Li Ling, Lü Xiang, and Guan Kai. Here I extend my especial thanks to these scholars.

I would also like to pay my respects to Su Bingqi, who contributed the idea of a "sky full of constellations" that not only describes the leg-endary state of Chinese civilization in the Neolithic era but also is an interpretive model of very profound thought. I will take it as a starting point for thinking about China. Xu Hong's idea of "the earliest China" is the starting point for another question. Given that the earliest China should be a formative process, there may not necessarily be a definite starting point as such, and yet, as a symbolic point of coalescence, the idea of the earliest China is still of significance. In this book, I set out a Chinese whirlpool as an interpretive model and use it to interpret China's growth, from the Shang and Zhou dynasties up to the Qing dynasty. The ancient stage of China where the sky is full of constellations ended in 1840, or perhaps 1900, when during the closing years of dynastic China there was a shift into the contemporary game. The main question is how ancient China became a virtually irresistible attraction from which, once one was drawn into the whirlpool game, it was difficult to withdraw. A second question is how the ontology of becoming and creative doing within the whirlpool became China's methodology.

Here I would also like to thank Wang Bin, Li Nan, and Wang Wenting of Zhongxin Press. They have put all their effort into the publishing of this book. I would also like to thank Zhao Tao, He Juling, and Wang Xing. In the journals they edit they have already published parts of this book. The artist Qiu Zhijie wrote the characters used for the title on the front cover of the original Chinese publication. I thank him for his friendship.

The Whirlpool that Produced China: Stag Hunting on the Central Plain (*Huici Zhongguo* 惠此中国), *The Contemporaneity of Tianxia*, and related topics of research have all benefited from the support of the Kaifeng Foundation and the Zhongxin Reform Development Foundation, to whom I express my thanks.

Zhao Tingyang
March 12, 2016

Introduction

If the history of a civilization has its own self-conscious trajectory of growth and internal motive force, and has made abstract time into a concrete historical self-consciousness and into an autonomous capacity and a model for creative doing—this kind of history then has historicity.[1] This sense of historicity is very close to the notions of "the way" (*dao* 道) and the "propensity of things" (*shi* 势) used to reference historical change in the way China conceives of history. Thus, we can say that history is the "doings" done by a civilization, and that historicity is the propensity of things that constitute the "way" of a civilization. The historicity of any civilization gives rise to three basic questions: Why is it like this? How did it come about? And what will it be like in the future? Paul Gauguin has a famous painting, the title of which expresses the same structure as these three questions: Where do we come from? Who are we? Where are we going?[2] These three questions help to explain each other. In fact, they can be combined into one question that draws together both ontology and the philosophy of history. How is an "existent" created? With respect to an entity that is self-conscious—such as a human society or a civilization—existence is no longer the natural existence of how something is as it is, but the historical existence of historicity. For this reason, the question of "being" is changed to become equivalent to the question of being made to be. "Making" or "doing" is to go and create a history of existence, that is, it ensures that an entity becomes a historical entity that cannot be reduced to the ordinary concept of mere existence.

The historical narration of doings is always a matter of subjective interpretation. Short of completely rejecting the human significance within the narration and writing a narrative for natural history or for zoological history, such subjectivity is inevitable. But to proceed in this

1

way amounts to failing to explain the historicity of human history and thus fails to say anything meaningful about life at all. It would definitely not be the history we try to understand. Indeed, historical interpretation is not a private pursuit, for it has guarantees relevant to a collective destiny. Thus, the subjectivity of historical narration must be restricted to an analytical framework that has objective constraints. This means that historical interpretation must chose—or acquiesce in—a philosophy. Principles that cannot be doubted are a priori in nature. However, historicity directly rejects the a priori. This is a problem, even a contradiction, though fortunately not a logical contradiction, and thus is not insoluble. Wittgenstein said that the way philosophy solves questions is precisely the same as how to show a fly the way out of the neck of the fly bottle.[3] The way out of the neck of the bottle that I hope to find for historicity is the constraint on ontology.

No form of existence can reject the purpose implied by existence itself. We may call this purpose the basic meaning of existence, that is, what existence itself must imply, or the demand that existence analytically implies. Analytical implication suggests a logical standard, namely, the rejection of any added meaning. That is, the nature that x necessarily implies is only deduced from the meaning of x itself. When analytical implication is used for ontology, we find that the basic meaning of existence is to continue to exist and nothing else. Therefore, we can say that to be is to be forever. Given that the narrative and the destiny of the existence of any historicity is accidental, we must then seek an eternal continuity that transcends history.[4] By virtue of their demand for ongoing continuity, all accidental narrations and their destiny have meaning.

In seeking to understand the many requirements of an existing entity, the demand for a constraint on ontology takes existence itself as the rule. When the ontological question is restricted to the question of the existence of human beings, existence is realized as "doing." Where there is no doing to be done, there is no existence. What doing seeks must be the greatest resources and profit that will be advantageous for an existing entity. Economics and game theory generally understand the greatest profit as referring to material profit. Material good confirms the root of life, but it cannot wholly express the demands of life. In fact, there are always some spiritual demands that are equally necessary, that is a spiritual life that one cannot do without, and for which one would prefer to die rather than suffer deprivation. Therefore, what is most advantageous and the greatest resource for an existing entity must be understood as the conjunction of both material and spiritual benefit, where there is a proportionate balance found between the two depending on what is best in the situation, and the changing circumstances.

In human life, a restraint on ontology is expressed concretely as human conduct being guided by rational choice. On the surface, events that are clamorous or that cause trouble are what are most evident in history. Hence, it is easy to produce a misapprehension that irrational conduct creates history. In fact, what is most advantageous to guaranteeing existence is rational conduct. This proceeds from the real meaning of existence. People usually select rational conduct. Reality shows that the means of production, technological discoveries, establishment of institutions, and the determination of norms and shaping of customs that have a long-lasting decisive influence on human life are the result of collective rational choice. According to Thomas Schelling and Ken Binmore, the doings that thus shape the human experience are all focal points produced by consistency in the choices made by human beings.[5] Therefore, rational conduct, far from being an incidental matter of mere words, is what is really needed to understand historical questions. Collective rational choice is a construction of historicity. Its rationality is expressed as a form of conduct that can be imitated and repeated. Only a form of conduct that can serve as a universal model and that is constantly repeated can shape the way of existence or, we might say, can shape the way of humankind over an extended period of time. What gives a form of conduct the status of serving as a constantly repeated universal model that is effective as a way of existence lies in the fact that it will not lead to resentment—to self-inflicted calamity. Or at least, with the tendency for producing resentment being at a minimum, it can shape a stable and ongoing historicity.[6]

If the history of a civilization is unable to respond to the question of its own historicity, this would mean that either it is unable to form its own independent historicity because its history lacks a sufficient capacity to interpret itself, or that it has lost historicity because there is no way to recover a history that has been terminated. This happens when its history has been subordinated to another guiding force, or when another history with a greater capacity obscures it. Clearly, the ability of a civilization to continue to exist lies in it having its own self-sufficient order of being, with this expression "order of being" coming from Eric Voegelin, from which it can shape a self-sufficient historicity, and is an order that cannot easily be deconstructed. A self-sufficient order of being must come from a home-grown and inner dynamic structure and be such that it can continue to operate without interruption. The question to be discussed here is: What is the inner dynamic structure that has shaped China's historicity?

China in terms of history and China in terms of geography are not exactly the same thing. On the piece of land that is called China today, various histories have occurred that do not fully belong to the concept of China. Some of these events, at certain times, have occurred on land that is China today, but they do not belong to the history of China. On the other hand, at certain times in history, some parts of China lie outside the territory of today's China. Although some areas no longer belong to modern China, what happened there does belong to Chinese history. For this reason, when we discuss the concept of China, it is difficult to avoid the problem of a confusion of nomenclature. Speaking of the realities of today, China is simultaneously a state, a civilization, and a history. But in terms of time, the China that is a state, the China that is a civilization, and the China that is a history did not all happen at the same time. Rather, they happened in stages and came together to produce this unity in the end. What force was it, and what destiny or cause brought it about that the China that is a state, the China that is a civilization, and the China that is a history coalesced into one rich concept? This narrative must have left some traces that we can pursue.

First of all, we need to clarify some concepts and the analytical framework. Xu Hong proposes the idea of "the earliest China" (zuizaode Zhongguo 最早的中国).[7] This is a concept that must be clarified; it is also a very meaningful question. In recent years there have been alternative proposals and many debates regarding the site of the earliest China. Currently there is no agreement, and we must wait upon further evidence. Perhaps from an archaeological point of view, the question of this site has real importance, but given the problem we wish to discuss here, the significance of the concept of the earliest China is what matters most, since it implies a starting point in terms of spirituality. The geographical site is merely of symbolic significance. First of all, we define the earliest China as the starting point of a Chinese civilization that can be recognized as Chinese. This, of course, does not refer to the earliest material objects or technological civilization found on Chinese soil. The first steps in China's technological civilization are several tens of thousands of years earlier, but such steps do not yet constitute a normative spiritual world. Hence, simply being able to say that some discovery on Chinese soil is the earliest civilization does not suffice to clarify the concept of the earliest China. Indeed, the concept of the earliest China must have a sufficiently discernible form and must suggest the propensity of China's growth, that is, it must already include the direction of China's growth.

I want to use the idea of Gestalt from Gestalt psychology to explain the formation of the concept of China, where "Gestalt" is very close to the Chinese idea of the "propensity of things" (*shi*). China is an entity that has been growing constantly. Even while not yet mature, it already had developed some basic spiritual principles and had formed the propensity toward a Gestalt. While still having space for further evolution, the propensity in the direction of the Gestalt already anticipated the concept of the whole. In order to attain its final form, China needed to meet at least the following three overlapping conditions: (1) The myriad peoples occupying the territory of China begin to have a commonly shared history. This commonly shared history does not preclude each ethnic group or political community having its own exclusive history outside the commonly shared history. The commonly shared history referenced here is a history created and shaped together at the place where their forking histories converged and is not a linear history forced unilaterally on others by one among them. (2) The foundation of the commonly shared history is a competitive game in which everyone takes part. And the peoples from the four quarters all have an interest in participating in this common game because of the benefits they can derive from it. (3) There are sufficient conditions to guarantee that this shared game of contest will continue to take place. The compounding of these three conditions can more or less anticipate the complete formation of the concept of China. At the same time, the Gestalt of Chinese civilization perhaps had to satisfy the coincidence of three conditions: (1) the first steps in the Gestalt formation of the basic principles of a spiritual world; (2) this spiritual world becoming the spiritual resource for which players in the game must contend; (3) this spiritual world having an open and shared nature where, because of this, it could serve as resource used by all. If the preceding conditions had not been met, the myriad people on Chinese soil could not have coalesced into one Chinese people, and the land of China could not have become China.

Chinese history in the geographical sense can be traced back to the Neolithic era. At that time in the region of China, from the Liao River, Mongolia, Qinghai, and Gansu to the Central Plain and the Yangtze River valley, there were many early civilizations that flourished contemporaneously with each other. Roughly speaking, this was the pattern of the "sky full of constellations" (*mantianxingdou* 满天星斗) suggested by Su Bingqi. This was a time of a plurality of forking histories that had not yet coalesced into one commonly shared history. Although there was interaction and movement among the civilizations of these various places, there was as yet no political game in which they all shared. They had not yet integrated into one common political order. The key lay in the fact that until a common game was formed, it was quite impossible to shape a common history or common political order. In other words, even if there were mutual exchanges in culture, news, and technology, this was not enough to give rise to a commonly shared history and a common polity because cultural exchange is not a sufficient condition for cultural unity. It was probably only in the beginning of the civilization of the three dynasties of the Xia, Shang, and Zhou that Chinese history truly formed its civilizational core and its centripetal force for growth. A key question to be explained is how the Central Plain became the core of the civilizational system toward which the various peoples turned. Xu Hong sees Erlitou as the earliest China. This is a very persuasive symbolic starting point. Erlitou may very well have taken the first steps in shaping the Gestalt of the concept of China, though further evidence is required. However, the China of the three dynasties is not the great, unified model of China. Rather it was a global *tianxia* (All under Heaven) world with "no beyond" (*wuwai* 无外). It was a *tianxia* system that, in theory, potentially included the myriad polities of the whole world, or said another way, it was a one-world political order. Even though China at that time was only part of the world, it was imagined to be the whole world and existed as a global structure. Thus, the history of the three dynasties is Chinese history, and yet at the same time it is world history. Strictly speaking, the world history of *tianxia* only belongs to the Zhou dynasty. The Xia and Shang may well have already possessed the *imaginaire* and outlook of *tianxia*, but they had not yet, in fact, established a *tianxia* order that was worldwide in nature. The legally determined order of the *tianxia* system was the creation of the Zhou dynasty. Even so, in a spiritual tradition that values the past, the name if not the fact of the *tianxia* order may be traced back to Yao and Shun, Tang and Wu, and even symbolically back to the Yellow Emperor. The idea of a large, unified China emerged in the Qin dynasty and was consolidated by the Han.[8] The Qin dynasty laid aside the old law of the *tianxia* order and replaced it with the organization of a great, unified state. From that time on, China's world history was over, and China's Chinese history began.

Although with the Qin and Han dynasties, the historical construct was no longer that of world history but was reduced to Chinese history, the great, unified China still retained the relics of the idea of *tianxia*, converting the spirit of *tianxia* into a national spirit, and reducing the world construct into a state construct. For this reason, China became a state that contained the structure of *tianxia*. This China that contained all of *tianxia* inherited the capacity for inclusiveness of the "no beyond" (*wuwai*) idea of *tianxia*. Or we might say that "no beyond" became an internalizing capacity. The sacredness of *tianxia* lies in its having an all-inclusive nature and in its being of the same structure as the all-inclusive heaven above. Therefore, the all-inclusive *tianxia* suffices to be a match with heaven.[9] Because the *tianxia* that is a match with heaven has the same structure as heaven, so also it is sacred. As the *Daodejing* says, "Matching heaven has been a principle since ancient times."[10] Precisely because China has the structure of *tianxia*, "China" became a sacred concept that could match heaven and was called the Sacred Continent. Mencius says, "What is full and brilliant is called 'great.' What is great and transforms things is called 'sagely.' What is sagely and cannot be known is called 'sacred.'"[11] The China that has the structure of *tianxia* cannot be reduced to being some commonplace national state or empire. The political implications of these latter notions in comparison with the China that has *tianxia* are far too simplistic, and even a category mistake.

There are three things about China that are taken to be virtually axiomatic. First, Chinese civilization is a civilization that has never been interrupted since the time it emerged. This supposes that Chinese civilization has a very strong sense of continuity. Second, Chinese civilization has always been constituted by many peoples and cultures. This supposes that Chinese civilization has a broad spectrum of inclusive compatibility. Third, Chinese civilization has not given rise to a universalist monotheism. At the most, it has some localized folk religions, most of which are not transcendental religions. For this reason, Chinese civilization is considered a highly secularized civilization that lacks religiosity. These axioms only give expression to phenomena, are based on a tacit deduction from such phenomena, and have not received a fully satisfactory interpretation. Therefore, I will try to turn these tacitly accepted axioms back into questions, not by doubting the phenomena that can be seen by all, but by seeking to explain why things are like this. At the same time, I will seek a novel understanding of these phenomena.

Rather than take the continuity, inclusive compatibility, and areligiosity of Chinese civilization as answers, it is much better to treat them as questions that need to be analyzed and explained. First of all, the key to why continuity and an inclusive compatibility came about lies in a motive force as its source. Why is it that Chinese civilization continues without interruption? Why is it inclusive? Clearly, the actual outcomes are not an explanation of the causes. If it was lacking in an irresistible and competitive gaming drive, then no game could possibly have been a continuing attraction. That a tradition can continue to exist is not because it is a tradition, but because there must be some kind of an objective drive with a certain degree of stability that makes it never want to stop. In the same way, the inclusive compatibility evident in a civilization cannot be wholly due to ethical ideas such as good intentions and tolerance—if ethics is unable to benefit humankind, people will lose any interest in ethics. Rather, there must be an irresistible drive toward benefit that causes them to all adopt a method of inclusiveness in which lies the greatest benefit for all. In sum, the reason why an entity exists as it does and the ultimate reason for its existence must be what gives the most benefit to its existential drive and the way it exists. This is the deepest reason why a tradition can become a tradition. Moreover, the reason for a survival based on ontology is especially helpful in understanding the subjective behavioral choices in history. We are unable to return to the past and survey the thoughts of the ancients. Rather than merely imagining what they might be like on the basis of our contemporary views on politics, if we take what interests are greatest for their survival as the starting point for understanding their choices, it at least allows the possibility of coming close to the truth of history. Understanding the ancients on the basis of what benefits their survival is a hermeneutical model that may help in clarifying many disputes dealing with the past: for instance, the disputes concerning the *New Qing History* and the *New Yuan History*. Why is it that the Yuan and Qing dynasties are Chinese royal dynasties? It has nothing to do with what people think today, but it is intimately related to what was of benefit for survival of the ancients. To become a Chinese dynasty is the most reliable guarantee for becoming lord of China. To guarantee the basis for lasting rule, the Yuan and Qing had to choose to become Chinese dynasties. Survival is the only certainty.

Therefore, I seek to explain the reasons by which China became China by taking the reasons of ontology and linking them with the methodology of game theory. I will argue that the gaming activities in which in early times the many peoples surrounding China on all four sides competed for the greatest material benefits and greatest spiritual resources produced a whirlpool model of drive that took the Central Plain as its core. Once the whirlpool was formed, it had an irresistible centripetal force that was self-strengthening, so much so that most participants not only had difficulty in withdrawing but did not want to withdraw. This ultimately led to a massive whirlpool that determined the scale of China's existence and made the concept of China real. The whirlpool model can explain why ancient China was not an expanding empire and yet did continue to expand. The secret for this is that the expansion of China was not due to the lure of loot gained through expansionist behavior but due to the gifts given by the surrounding contenders as they were constantly being drawn into the core of the whirlpool. The formation of the Chinese whirlpool has, on the one hand, to do with the game of contending for the core and, on the other, with inventing the order of *tianxia*. The *tianxia* order was able to dissolve the fierce contention for the whirlpool and to ensure acceptance of the common institutions of the myriad peoples. It created the common model of many cultures and many peoples, and it created the model of one system with many forms of governance. Even after the end of the *tianxia* system, the *tianxia* spirit was a legacy that was transformed into the internal structure of China as a state. Thus, it was able to shape a great unified country of many cultures and peoples. In fact, what is meant by the unified rule is a state that has *tianxia* as its internal structure.

Precisely because China's inner structure always maintained the *tianxia* construct of being a match with heaven, China became a sacred entity, a belief. This can answer the question of China's spiritual belief. Any civilization requires some kind of spiritual belief. It is where the civilization settles and lives out its destiny and is the basis for its confirmation of itself. Generally people think that China lacked a religion in the strict sense and so lacked a spiritual belief.[12] This understanding is very much open to question. If China truly lacked a spiritual belief, then how can we explain the wholeness and stability of the Chinese spirit? This is a mystery that has never yet been satisfactorily resolved. The more common explanation is to take Confucianism as a proto-religion to explain the consistency of the Chinese spirit, but this explanation clearly cannot fully explain the whole spiritual world of China. Maybe an appeal to Confucianism can roughly explain the social structure and lifestyle of ancient China, but it has difficulty in explaining China's spiritual belief because what Confucianism establishes are ethical principles. If ethics is said to be what constitutes religion, then it is hard to avoid a confusion of terms. In Chinese culture, there is no covenant model between human beings and God, and so there is indeed no religion in the Western sense. However, there are other types of belief, such as the congruity between the human way and the way of heaven, and of being a match with heaven. Any entity that attains a match with heaven is a sacred entity and becomes a belief. The reason why China's spiritual belief is hidden and not manifest is because it is tacit and unknown. In fact, China's spiritual belief is China itself. In other words, China is the spiritual belief of Chinese people. The China that is a match with heaven as its principle is the sacred idea of China.

I would like to interpret the structure of China's historicity as a way of paying respect to the ancestors. The construction of historicity means inviting the contemporaneity of the past time to become present again and to engage with the contemporaneity of the present time so as to understand how the contemporaneity of the past foreshadows, or prepares the way for, the contemporaneity of the present. This is to narrate the past so as to show respect for the ancestors.

Chapter One

A Whirlpool Model of China

Writing about China is harder than writing about *tianxia*. In the *tianxia* of the Western Zhou there were states, and in the states there were families. *Tianxia* was the order of the world; the traditions of each state were the norms of each place. The China of unified rule of the post-Qin-Han times, however, is a state that contains the structure of *tianxia*, bringing together into one the lands all around, making the myriad peoples into one family. There is the sense of *tianxia* but the reality of one state. Hence a political form is created whereby the format of a limited state expresses the unlimited idea of *tianxia*. Simultaneously, a mental construct was created such that the state was the body and *tianxia* was the way. As a result Chinese people looked at the infinite from within the finite. A way of observing was shaped such that those living within a limited territory reminisced over a space with no borders. This gave rise to the question of how the structure of the state and the structure of *tianxia* could come together, in what form, and how was it formed? This is an important issue for understanding the way in which China exists.

Before we analyze the motive for the growth and continuity of China, we must first of all clarify some background ideas that will help in shaping the discussion of Chinese historical periods. The *tianxia* system of the Zhou was weakened in the Spring and Autumn period and wiped out in the Qin. The pre-Qin era is that of China's *tianxia* period that applies to both Chinese history and world history as well. This was a preparatory period in the formation of a unified China. The First Emperor of Qin founded the unified system of commanderies and counties, bringing the many states within the territory that is now China into one state.[1]

On the one hand, he established the tradition of a great, unified state; on the other, this led to the notion of *tianxia* becoming reduced to that of China. In terms of world history, *tianxia* was finished; the story of *tianxia* was reduced to the story of China. The period from the Qin to the Qing is that of ancient China. After 1911, China tried to copy the European model of the nation-state and establish a modern, sovereign country, while also holding on to something of the national tradition of ancient China. This resulted in a complex construct that did not fully realize the structure of a country. The way in which China has existed, as described here, does not include modern China.

While the unification brought about by the Qin ended the *tianxia* system, yet the same idea still functioned as a political gene in the reality of the Chinese state. Even though, since the Qin-Han era, China no longer aspired to bring about *tianxia* governance on the world level, yet it still sought to run itself as a reduced version of *tianxia*, with the measure of *tianxia* confined to China. These two forms of politics each have their own goal. The ultimate aim of running *tianxia* was to internalize the whole world. There would be nothing external to the world in which all peoples would enjoy one society, and all political bodies should be harmonized within the framework of *tianxia*, "the myriad states in harmony."[2] The chief goal of running China was to allow the China that bore the nature of *tianxia* to continue to exist in perpetuity, without worrying anymore about how to internalize the world. Therefore, the outside world became a lasting challenge. Already, in Zhou times, "the tributary barbarians did not come."[3] This was the result of what was regarded as a mistake by King Mu of Zhou.[4] From Qin-Han times onward, whenever the nomadic peoples did not see the people of the Central Plain as their enemies, there was peace and the state was better off. As the understanding of there being nothing external to *tianxia* receded, what was internal and what external to the state became the focus. In the attempt to ensure China would become a state that could meet any game challenge from outside, concentration on how to run China centered on setting up a lasting and stable internal order. Holding on to territory became the main duty. The original ideal of there being nothing external to *tianxia* was "treating *tianxia* as one family; treating China as one person."[5] With the ending of the Zhou system of *tianxia*, the ideal of there being nothing external was limited to the second phrase in this quotation. It became the principle of the accommodation of diversity within China. Yet, this principle itself retained the genes of *tianxia*, and the China that retained within itself the structure of *tianxia* was a political reality.

The dual nature of China as having national identity and *tianxia* determined that ancient China was always an idea in progress, one that was also always open and yet could expand or contract. *Tianxia* is the universal order equally good for all peoples in the world and not a form of imperialism under one ruling city or state. China existed as a constantly evolving notion, like the "change" of the *Book of Changes*. While many changes may occur, what remains unchanging is the fact of change itself. Thus "China" is a way of growth, not an unchanging concept. Its actual realization was always changing, reaching its largest compass in the Han, Tang, Yuan, and Qing dynasties, while under the Sixteen Kingdoms, Northern and Southern Dynasties, Five Dynasties and Ten Kingdoms, and the Song, Liao, Jin, and Xia, it was divided. Since the Qin-Han era, China has been divided for slightly longer than it has been united, yet unification has always remained a dogma of political theology. As a historical phenomenon, China is a dynamic process of division and reunion, with division and reunion following in a constant cycle. Yet, the reunion during its periods of unification is always what gives meaning to its existence and is its essential goal. Unification is not only a search for political power; it is also an economic necessity that allows for the myriad people to live together in peace. Provided that security and stability can be guaranteed, the resources of a large state—the diversity of its economy, the way different parts complement each other, and the size of the population—are all an enormous asset. This is the economic advantage that lies behind the political reality of unification. According to the ontology of the *Book of Changes*, "generation and regeneration" is the basic reason for existence. A political environment that allows for all things and all people to generate and regenerate is a reasonable environment in which to exist. While the dogma of unification has its attraction, it still requires that an objective impulse and a model of operation have their determinative role before it can become a reality. So the dogma of unification itself is not sufficient to explain the continuity and cohesiveness of China. There must be some other irresistible objective impulse. It is this issue that must be analyzed.

It is very difficult for the historical accounts of people today to avoid the interpellation of reflections based on today's way of thinking. Even though what is so today may give rise to new questions with respect to what was so in the past, yet we must not allow what is so today to falsify what was so in the past. To do this would be to be anachronistic. To allow the ideas of today to be reflected and subsequently confirmed as ancient facts is a form of reverse construction that will sever the natural arteries of history and destroy the irreversible continuity of time and place. History then becomes an accretion of unlinked impressions and loses its own continuous historicity. For instance, the modern academic ideas of the nation-state, nationalism, dynastic succession, and imperialism are deeply rooted in accounts of Western history and are of course relevant to that history. But when used to explain the Chinese narrative, they break the thread of history. This is deconstruction rather than explanation; it is to wipe out rather than to give an account of history. While the story of China after 1911 has, to a large extent, become a part of a Western-directed history—for example, how China today is in some way being reborn—yet, if China's story is constructed in reverse along Western lines, it will simply lead to equivocation and misunderstanding.

The spiritual world of China arose in shamanism and matured in historical consciousness. This is something all historians recognize. In the words of Chen Mengjia, it is the development of "history out of shamanism."[6] Or, as Zhang Guangzhi has shown, at the dawn of Chinese civilization the shaman, who had a form of power that can be interpreted as spiritual, and the king, who was a political leader, were combined as one. This implies that spiritual power was important for political power. When Chinese characters appeared, the graph *shi* 史 (history/historian) had a much stronger spiritual sense than it does today. Hence the identities of the historian and the shaman were once combined in one person.[7] Li Zehou observes that the key to Chinese civilization was how in the spiritual tradition shamanism was transformed into history and finally led to historical awareness. He calls it the "shamanic history tradition."[8] We might infer that once historical awareness had acquired explanatory force in interpreting the mode of existence, China's reflection on existence became a philosophy of history. "Being" was "becoming." And becoming was to change time into history. Therefore, the tenses used for being are the progressive and future tenses. By way of contrast, from the time of ancient Greece, the way Western thought has reflected on being has been conceptual. Being must exist as an eternal concept. As a result, the tense for existence is the ordinary present tense. In the spiritual world of China, history is the yardstick. The entire meaning of being unfolds in history. The statement that the "Six Classics are all history" means precisely this.[9]

For Confucius, an understanding of the *Spring and Autumn Annals* had to express the overarching meaning of history and the reason why things were so; how the human way must match the way of heaven, what he called "being a match with heaven." All historical accounts based on an understanding of this "matching up with heaven" orthodoxy were acceptable. All kinds of orthodox interpretations could be used to support a historical point of view. However, what served as an orthodox argument could not be some subjective, self-referential account, nor could it be some self-repeating discourse. If such were the case, the argument would fail. That is to say, even where words could express the overarching meaning, that meaning could not authenticate itself. Sima Qian's consciousness of the unity that runs through change may sound more sober, but it gets much closer to the nature of historical change itself, and to the way that existential changes take place. On this point, I do not intend to argue in favor of any particular orthodox view as being definitive but to just limit myself to analyzing what kind of collective historical movement led to the formation of China. This is but to say that I will not try to understand the evolution of China by appealing to the values advanced by historians but rather try to understand how China became what it is through the choices made by historical actors trying to gain the greatest benefit in their competitive game. China's process of growth may be understood as a lengthy, continuous game. Interpreters all have their own value judgments about the historical alterations of loss and gain within the game, but the key to what actually made China what it is lies, in the end, in the rational choices made by historical actors. It is the collective behavior of actors that defined the problems, the purposes, and the nature of the game. There are two key questions that relate to the outlook of the historical actors. First, China being a continuously existing entity, what was the nature of the motive force that gave impetus to China's continuity? Second, since the dominant gene that is most advantageous to existence will be continually repeated, what then is the gene of existence that has continually been repeated in Chinese history? What I am referring to is the thought gene that has governed the collective behavioral choices—in other words, their mindset.

In all parts of the world, different historical conditions have led to many different ways in which history has run its usual course. Early

Chinese politics began with world politics, that is, with *tianxia* as the world order, and they sought to found a state within this order. Western politics, however, began with a small model of political space, the polis, that was defined by matters of shared public life. These two political models seek to address different questions, yet both are directed at resolving the basic issues of human life. Whether the political genes differ or whether they complement each other, they cannot be treated as being of the same kind. Rather they delineate a political territory wherein each can mutually enrich the other. History has shown that these two political traditions have proved to be the longest lasting political modes of governance, and given the current state of globalization, these two political traditions might be combined into one new form of politics.[10]

Since the Qin-Han era, China has adopted a state politics, yet one that is a long way from the Western notion of a state. China is not a polis, nor is it a nation-state, nor is it an empire in the Western sense of this term. Even though ancient China does have some external similarities such as frontiers rather than clear boundaries that seem to be like those of an empire, while perhaps alike in external appearances it is wholly other in spirit.[11] While ancient China might look like an empire, it lacked the desire to expand that characterizes imperialism and is its defining feature. While China certainly did on occasion expand, yet it was very rare for there to be any active urge for it to expand and for any such actions to be undertaken. The many instances of large-scale expansion were all by-products of defensive measures taken to stave off attacks. The territorial expansion during the Han, Tang, and Qing dynasties were mainly the result of counterattacks for self-defense.[12] This suggests that expansion was not the rationale for China's existence as a state, nor was it a motive for the way in which it conducted its matters of state. Perhaps ancient China could be defined as a "leading power," but such a vague idea cannot fully express the true political nature of China.[13] There is another view that China differs from nation-states in being a civilization-state.[14] Currently, this view is widely held in both China and the West. It is certain that China is not a nation-state, but to define China as a civilization-state is liable to lead to misunderstanding. If a civilization can define China, why cannot other civilizations define other states? What could other civilizations be lacking that would preclude them being defined in this way? Again, how should the multiethnic states of Russia, India, and the United States of America be understood? The key issue is that by using a nation to define a state makes it possible to express its political nature in a clear way, whereas given that "civilization" is a term that includes everything, using it to define a state makes it difficult to express its political nature with the same degree of clarity. It is hard to imagine what cultural or social characteristics would not be included. Whatever the case, a state is a political entity and hence the definition as a state can do justice to the contours of its political nature. If we try to understand China from an anthropological point of view rather than from its politics, then Wang Mingming's "civilization body" (*wenmingti* 文明体) is better than that of a civilization-state.[15]

The reason that China is different from a nation-state must be due to China's political concept: the notion of *tianxia* as China's political gene, and the basic principles of "being a match for heaven" (*peitian* 配 天) having "no beyond" (*wuwai* 无外) and its "compatibility" (*xiehe* 协 和). From this we can say that China is a microcosm of *tianxia*; it is a state that takes *tianxia* as its internal structure. If we must take the nation-state as the corresponding idea, then the China that includes the *tianxia* nature may perhaps be called an "inclusive state." This concept only applies to ancient China. China today has a dual nature: its traditional Chinese identity to which has been added a notion of a modern state. On the basis of the genes of ancient China, modern China has brought in the modern state and become a modern sovereign state, but it is still not a nation-state. The dispute over the nature of modern China is in fact due to a narrow understanding of the nation-state, namely, that a modern state must be a nation-state. In practice, there are at least two basic types of modern sovereign states: the nation-state (such as the states of Europe), and the multiethnic state (such as the United States, China, Russia, and India).[16] Multiethnic states have the legally defined boundaries and sovereignty that are the basic attributes of the modern nation-state, but they differ from the nation-state in that they have many peoples and cultures. Based on the current tendency, more and more nation-states are slowly evolving into multiethnic states. The rapid increase of Arabs, Africans, Eastern Europeans, and East Asians in many European countries means that it is difficult to say that there is a nation-state in the original sense. Therefore, the multiethnic state may well develop to become the main type of modern state. From this it can be seen that, in terms of geography and history, the nation-state is not the mainstream type of modern state. Rather it is something that emerged in one corner of the world—Europe—at one particular time—the Thirty Years' War.

To return to our main theme, because the politics of China also includes the gene of *tianxia*—even when *tianxia* was realized only in China—ancient China lacked any positive quest to be a nation-state or to pursue nationalism. It was only in the late Qing, when China encountered the challenge of the modern Western nation-state, that there arose the idea of being strong like a nation-state and adopting nationalism. Liang Qichao was probably the first to suggest the appropriating of Western nationalism and the nation-state in order to change the country into a modern sovereign state.[17]

Ancient China did not have the idea of sovereignty; it only had the reality of political power. It had no legally defined borders. What it called the territory under its rule was merely a mathematical function derived from actual power. Ancient wars were not nationalist wars but wars over political authority, a "stag hunt" (*zhulu* 逐鹿) for power. The general of the Liao army that fought against the Song, Han Derang, was a Han Chinese. So too was the general of the Yuan army that over-threw the Song, Zhang Hongfan. If the notion of modern nationalism is taken as the measure, then they would be reckoned as traitors. But in the historical language of the day they were residents of the northern dynasties where they were born and grew up, and the northern dynasties were also Chinese, just as Song was a southern dynasty of China. It was simply that Zhang Hongfan believed that heaven's mandate lay with the Yuan while Wen Tianxiang believed that orthodoxy lay with the Song.

If the cause of division and unification of ancient China had nothing to do with race, then what was it? How was this historical impetus shaped? China is a land that brings "the myriad peoples of the four quadrants" together, or perhaps is a multiethnic state in today's language. Chinese history is also the product of the concerted efforts of these myriad peoples. It is a tale woven with many threads. Each thread is a history that ensures the continuity of history and may have some basic problems or some kinds of events that are constantly repeated. But what is it then that causes similar problems and events to constantly recur? The simplest explanation is to attribute it all to tradition. The constant, unbroken existence of China is commonly attributed to the Chinese cultural tradition, frequently called the Confucian tradition. The Confucian tradition is said to have a marked ethical superiority. There are some doubts that arise from this kind of cultural mythology. First, then, what are the historical realities that prove the moral superiority of the Chinese people? This is a problem. I am afraid that we cannot overlook the gap between moral teachings and actual behavior.[18] We should realize the collective behavior that in fact constitutes history arises from a much stronger reason and motive force. Second, Confucian ideas only began to gradually attain the status of supreme authority after the Song, and it was especially only in the Ming and Qing that they held sway over a person's whole life as moral teachings. By that time, the current model of China was already in place. This implies that the way in which the idea or existence of China came to be must be due to some other reason. Confucianism is, without doubt, the most important tradition in China, but the variety of Chinese traditions is also a manifest reality. Daoism, Buddhism, and Legalism have had a great influence that should not be overlooked. A further question to be asked is: Even if we suppose tradition to have sufficient hermeneutic force regarding history, nonetheless at the spiritual level it is only a superficial attitude and does not provide an adequate explanation. We still need to ask why this kind of tradition should arise, why people are faithful to it, and wherein the tradition's ongoing force of attraction lies. Why too does a tradition have limits with respect to its cultural borders and its proliferation?

Historical events are merely a story; behind the story there is always the structure of the motive impulse internal to its history. The question that needs to be explained is what is the motive impulse that gives rise to the constant repetition of any given thing? There is no doubt that historical events are accidental happenings and have a creative aspect, and that they are subject to many complex changes. The direct cause for any happening may be a one-time conflict over some interest, or a long period of accumulated resentment, or an accidental act of kindness to an enemy, or a difficulty brought about by a natural disaster, or a scheme born of ambition, or something else of the same kind. Yet accidental causes cannot explain the long-term motive impulse that results in history continually repeating itself. The key to the inevitability of history must lie in the structure of the motive impulse that lies behind the constant repetition found in a narrative of twists and turns. It is this inherent structure of the motive impulse that constantly gives rise to the same kind of ongoing collective behavior and that defines what kind of game a history is. Since historicity as such is not directly expressed in the narrative of history, but lies hidden in the antinarrative of the historical narrative, it can only be seen in what is constantly repeated within events that cannot themselves be repeated. History as such is metaphysical or ontological in nature and thus can explain why something is what it is, and why it persists in this way. When, within the temporality of a given moment, history as such is constructed by a structure of motive impulse that is aware of itself, then history takes possession of time, or said differently, time becomes history. The key to the issue is what manner of motive, or motive impulse then, can convert time into history? There are many ways in which historicity can be understood: as a transcendental theology, as a natural theology, or as a political theology, or some such. If history is construed as a preordained ultimate goal, then historicity as such is a mission. If it is understood as a process of limitless development, then historicity as such is a way by which existence seeks to perpetually grow itself. The latter is the disposition of Chinese historicity. It is a way of growth in which the future leads the way. Its origins are in generation and regeneration and the daily renewal set out in the *Book of Changes*.[19]

The direct impulse for growth is always a matter of seeking after resources for existence. This is a natural state of affairs. When people seek a stable, reliable, long-lasting existence, in trying to foretell the future, they must also seek political resources, and hence they enter into a political state of affairs. The initial step in the search for existence is an economic issue, but lest the future be taken away by others, the next step is a political issue. The mere economic activity of sustaining existence is a relationship between humans and nature alone. It pertains to natural processes and does not yet constitute history. It is confined to temporality rather than historicity as such. As soon as relations of interest give rise to problems of power then one enters into the competitive game of humans with humans. In this sense, history always begins with politics. Power implies the establishment of order. It entails the transformation of openly accessible resources into exclusively controlled resources in order that the continuation of existence may be reliably expected. It might be said that politics is the attempt to establish some kind of order whereby to possess the future. When an order tries to determine what must happen in the future then it is creating history. Hence, we can understand Eric Voegelin's statement, "The order of history comes from the history of order."[20]

When a historical order (that is also a political and a theological order since they are frequently one and the same) becomes a political resource that everyone seeks after, then it will give rise to a competitive game in which all participate and from which develops their collective history. When a historical order or a competitive game becomes an objective of collective interest for many peoples, it becomes a focal point of history and politics. The term "focal point" is borrowed from the game theory of Thomas C. Schelling. A focal point is the choice of optimal benefit for the players even though they have not discussed it or agreed upon it in advance.[21] Here, "focal point" can be used to explain the formation of a common history. The question then, with respect to China, is what kind of historical order and what kind of competitive game made China's history into the common history of many peoples?

There was once a common understanding—it is hard to determine who first suggested it—that China was formed by constant expansion and propagation from the Central Plain to the surrounding areas. Zhang Guangzhi noted early on that this view of expansion outward from the Central Plain was mistaken. Rather, it was the result of mutual interchange between the civilizations of each locality. What occasioned this misunderstanding of China's growth was that, because archaeological interest focused on the Central Plain and the excavations of the center appeared to be far more than those from other places, this evidence "supported the mistaken view of the Central Plain as the core."[22] Later, with more digs being carried out elsewhere, people came to realize that the four lands around China—Qinghai and Gansu to Xinjiang in the west, Mongolia and Manchuria in the north, the Yangtze River valley in the south, and Shandong in the east—had civilizations that were equal or nearly equal to those of the Central Plain. In terms of material technology and the designs on objects, there were many similarities among the regions, indicating that there were many exchanges among the civilizations. Although exchange among these ancient civilizations is a fact, yet the reason behind it is a mystery. The only means of travel was by foot, and even though the distance between these civilizations was only several hundred *li*, in terms of the time it would take to go from one place to another, they were as far away as the ends of the earth. While contact between them was possible, it is unclear what motive there could be for expending the effort to travel. In short, in the Neolithic era, there were many civilizations in China and they interacted with each other, but each one had its own unique characteristics. It was not as if "one was a variant of another."[23] Hence, what Su Bingqi describes as "a sky full of constellations" is perhaps a more accurate description of early China before the Xia, Shang, and Zhou dynasties.

From the Xia, Shang, and Zhou dynasties onward, the Central Plain did indeed become the core of China. The basic question is how to understand the nature of this core and the relationship between the core and its four surrounding areas. In other words, the fundamental question is to explain how China became a whole entity that included the Central Plain and the surrounding areas. In the process of the formation of China, there was indeed the twin natural occurrences of interchange among the regional cultures, and again the expansion and spread of the center to the peripheries. Both sociology and anthropology suppose that people have a natural propensity to interact with each other. But the phenomenon of these two natural occurrences—or perhaps they were only accidental occurrences—is still insufficient to give rise to any deeper explanation of China's manner of growth. On the one hand, intercommunication itself cannot be a sufficient explanation for the formation of China as a whole because communication among the different cultures would not necessarily lead to their merging into one. It would be equally possible for each to take what it needed from the other and retain their own distinctive traits. It could even be that interaction would lead to the possibility of rejection and enmity between them. On the other hand, the model of the center extending outward is drawn from Western history, and it has a low degree of applicability to the reality of China's long history. Hence, it may well not be the chief cause of China's existence as a whole. It is not easy to explain Chinese history using Western models because the dissimilarities in the growth of these two histories are greater than their similarities. The reliable basis for expansion is military conquest, without which it cannot succeed. The ancient Central Plain was the first area to enter an agricultural way of life, and military force was not its strong point: "The Divine Farmer could not conquer."[24] However, the Central Plain was the treasured land that the peoples of the four surrounding areas came to conquer. The surrounding peoples were constantly coming together in this region, and thus began the "stag hunt" on the Central Plain with the result that there was a large-scale amalgamation of peoples. This was the main historical fact. The earliest accounts of "stag-hunting" battles on the Central Plain are the engagements at Banquan and at Zhuolu recorded in the ancient histories. These were also milestone events in the blending of the various Chinese peoples. The tribe of the Yellow Emperor that was constituted of nomadic hunters[25] defeated the agricultural tribe of the Fiery Emperor and the fishermen and hunters of Chi You's people, bringing renown to the Yellow Emperor.[26] In this way, the traditional account of an early cooperative order was established. The various peoples were absorbed into one and thus came to define the legendary idea of a Chinese people known as the children of the Yellow and Fiery Emperors. From this we can see that the earliest idea of the Chinese people was of nomadic pastoralists (hunters), agriculturalists, and fishermen-hunters coming together on the Central Plain. If we suppose that the era of the Yellow Emperor was really, as recounted in legends, around five thousand years ago, then at that time there was still no classically defined nomadic or agricultural life. There must have been a diverse economy where each emphasized one more than the other.[27] An even more important question is that, even where there is expansion, there is no guarantee that unity will be preserved. In fact, it is even more probable that there will be division, even defeat in war. Historical facts show that attacks on the powerholders of the Central Plain were frequent occurrences. It is thus clear that the growth of China must be due to some factor other than expansion from the Central Plain. Such expansion has no persuasive force in explaining the growth of China.

In theory, the root cause that can guarantee the formation of a large-scale political and cultural entity can only be some irresistible force of attraction, what was described by Confucius as "those nearby rejoice in it; those far away repair to it."[28] This is the reason I choose the focal point as a model to explain the way China grew. There must have been some irresistible force of attraction that led China to become the collective choice of many peoples on all four sides. There are many focal points in Chinese history that deserve study. Here we will analyze just one political competitive game as a focal point that runs through China's ancient history: that is, the game in which the Central Plain was the core of a "stag hunt" for *tianxia*, and in which the structure of the motive force sustaining the continuity of this game was a strong centripetal, whirlpool model. Many relevant actors were unable to resist the tempting benefits of this whirlpool and continued as major players to enter into the game and become competitors for lordship over China. There were also many related actors who were passively drawn into the game. The scope of the whirlpool gradually expanded and the centripetal force increased until it stabilized to become the large China, defined in terms of the Chinese whirlpool. This Chinese whirlpool is the core question that must be analyzed and explained.

In geographical terms, in the large area from the northern deserts to south of the Yangtze, from the East Sea to the western regions, an undivided space for the "stag hunt" was formed. The core locale of this broad area is commonly called the Central Plain. It is the area where China first develops due to geographical and climactic conditions, and to convenience for transport. This was not only the earliest economic and political center but also the center of culture. As such, it was the place where the "stag hunt" for *tianxia* was fought and decided. The expression "stag hunting on the Central Plain" (*zhongyuanzhulu* 中原 逐鹿) captures the competitive game of Chinese history in a dramatic way. Zhao Hui holds that this expression is effective in reflecting the mainstream, dynamic trajectory of Chinese history that took the Central Plain as its core.[29] Let us suppose that all competitors with a given strength are interested in the inherent and long-term benefits of the "stag hunt" on the Central Plain, then the next question necessary for further explanation is: Why is it that the game of "stag hunting" on the Central Plain was not merely a matter of victory or defeat, success or failure, by invading armies, but became a whirlpool model that players not only did not want to leave, but that they could not quit? Why is it that "stag hunting" on the Central Plain could produce a centripetal force that brought about a greater union of all? Why is it that the strong were not content to simply cleave a slice away for each to gain a portion of wealth and power on the scales of a game of competition? To put it bluntly, the real question is: What were the special, superior resources of the Central Plain that were unrivaled and had to be fought for?

Zhang Guangzhi believes that in China "the civilizational impetus is a combination of politics and wealth."[30] That is certainly so, but that politics seeks wealth is a commonplace and, as the ordinary state of affairs, cannot do justice to the special case of China. In this respect, China does not seem to provide any kind of an outstanding example. Even though the material civilization of the Central Plain along the middle reaches of the Yellow River may have had a relatively combined superiority—many people are happy to think as much—yet it did not seem to have been an overriding advantage, nor was it the case that the various technologies available to it were the best. Archaeological evidence shows that in early China, from Inner Mongolia and Liaoning in the north to the Yangtze River basin in the south, there are sites of the origins of many civilizations all nestled closely together. In terms of resources, each had its own products, and each also relied on the others. With respect to technological ability, they were all very close though each had its specialty. In terms of the material standard of living, they were all very similar. And the size of their populations was not that different.

Why then is it that they were not satisfied with remaining where they were but felt compelled to join the "stag hunt" on the Central Plain? Even if we suppose that the material wealth of the ancient Central Plain was, relatively speaking, slightly superior, it would not be a sufficient difference to explain why the Central Plain became the "stag" in the hunt after which they would all chase and risk everything in doing so. War is a huge gamble in terms of treasure, and it is a risky adventure. Rationally speaking, no one would be willing to risk its dangers. This being the case, the Central Plain must have constituted a huge, irresistible temptation. Otherwise it is hard to explain why the Central Plain became the land for which the leading powers had to contest.

What is it about the Central Plain that makes it a superior resource that is unmatched and for which all must contend? Clearly, this requires our further investigation. Material wealth and hubs of communication are without doubt important factors in the balance, but they would not appear to be decisive. That is, they are not irreplaceable to the extent that they cannot be given up. Perhaps we should analyze other possibilities besides material conditions, among them being a spiritual world that constitutes a temptation with a great magical attraction. This differs from the consumptive nature of the material world. The spiritual world is appreciative, with its efficacy incremental and limitless. The more widely a spiritual world is used, the more people share in it and, as a consequence, it accumulates more and more cultural value-added and political magic that is hard to resist. As a result, it can attract more and more hearts with the result that a circle of infinitely increasing value will be created. Thus, there is reason to believe that the special status of the Central Plain must lie in the fact that it had a spiritual world imbued with added political value, a spiritual world of a political power that everyone could join and take as their own, gain from, hold on to, and expand. It was this spiritual world that was especially worth contending for in the "stag hunt." The reason the spiritual world of the Central Plain had the power to rally competitors and was a source of universal joy must be due, at least in part, to the following:

(1) The written Chinese characters. This was the form of writing developed early on the Central Plain and at the time may have been the most mature form of writing in the world.[31] Already by around four thousand years ago they had become a digital system capable of recording and storing a large amount of information and also a vector of writing capable of carrying complex thought and rich narratives. Hence, they led

the way in having the capacity to structure a spiritual world. Therefore, the spiritual world sustained in Chinese characters meant that early China developed, before any other place, a large-scale communicative capacity and information system. What is especially noteworthy is that Chinese characters began as hieroglyphs and not as marks for recording spoken phonemes. This suggests that the spoken language of the Central Plain could not have sole ownership over Chinese characters. In other words, it was possible for Chinese characters to be independent of the spoken language of the Central Plain and become a spiritual vector that could be enjoyed universally. Therefore, in essence, Chinese characters are a universally available resource that is open to all. Since all other peoples, using other languages, could possess and enjoy their use, the spiritual world sustained by Chinese characters became a spiritual resource that could be enjoyed universally.

(2) A system of thought. Fortified by the maturity of Chinese characters, the culture of the Central Plain developed to become a system of thought with a hermeneutical and reflective capacity of the greatest compass in its time. It could be used to explain the myriad happenings in the world, along with providing a worldview and historical outlook for human life and politics. The fruits of that early thought are gathered, preserved, and expressed in the classical canons: the *Book of Changes*, the *Book of History*, the *Rites of Zhou*, the *Book of Odes*, and the *Spring and Autumn Annals*. A profoundly reflective way of thinking implies that the thought system of the Central Plain in the early period already possessed the capacity to organize space on a large scale and to manage time; in other words, it was historical in nature and also public. That is to say, it had an extensive capacity for organizing society and creating order. At the same time, it provided the resources for orthodox self-awareness in interpreting history, society, order, and power. Thus, it naturally became the spiritual resource of optimal benefit for China at the time.

(3) The *tianxia* system created by the Zhou dynasty was also a determining factor. The principle of nonexclusion of the *tianxia* idea implies the maximum degree of accommodation. Since no one is precluded from taking part, it promises the model of a competitive game in which everyone can participate. Because of this, it had an equal force of attraction for all and could likewise be a political resource that had utility for everyone. Compatible with this, the Zhou idea of "the mandate of heaven" (*tianming* 天命) took "having virtue" as the justification for gaining *tianxia*. This amounted to arguing for the legitimacy

of revolution; hence, the idea of the "stag hunt" rose to eminence. The idea of *tianxia* is a potent example of how what is particular in nature can be transformed into what is universal. Although the notion of *tianxia* was the particular invention of the Zhou, yet the content of this idea excludes none and has universal meaning. It was for this reason that it could be universally accepted to become a political theological resource that can be enjoyed universally.[32]

(4) The snowball effect of political theology. To maintain a stable hold on and legitimate use of the optimal benefits provided by their spiritual and material resources, the victors in the "stag hunt" for the most part all rationally chose the mythology of the transmission of the mandate of heaven created by the Zhou dynasty to explain their own narratives of rulership. They would place their own dynasty into the long story of political succession that began with the Yellow Emperor to become one chapter in this multivolume story and with it, to explain their political legitimacy. This was the lowest cost strategy for winning political legitimacy and also the strategy that yielded the highest benefit. It is difficult to think that any victor in the "stag hunt" could reject this political theology. Therefore, this historical thread, constantly enriched by later narratives, became a political theology in which all believed. Not only did it become a ready-made advantageous resource that would be hard to abandon but, at the same time, it virtually closed the door on the possibility of any new historical narrative. The cost of rejecting a deeply rooted and vibrant historical theology and constructing a completely new historical theology was too high. The task would be too great, and the effort to justify oneself would amount to setting a course fraught with every kind of difficulty and failure.

Perhaps there are further considerations, but the aforementioned determining factors were already sufficient to produce the whirlpool model of "stag hunting" on the Central Plain. The key to the whirlpool effect lies in its continuous centripetal force. History shows that the earliest political powers that fought for the optimal benefits and actively entered into the "stag hunting" game on the Central Plain thereby produced the beginnings of the whirlpool. As more political powers joined in, the volume of the whirlpool continually grew larger. The significance of its spiritual resources and its political theology continually increased, thus further reinforcing the centripetal force of the whirlpool. It is the whirlpool effect created by the ongoing game of "stag hunting" for *tianxia* that created China and the Chinese whirlpool model of growth.

The open-endedness of this whirlpool game—derived from the idea of *tianxia*—determined that China would be an idea that would constantly grow, with no perceptible limit to this growth. It would be an idea of China that would draw ever closer to the measure of *tianxia*.

Chapter Two

The China That Contains *Tianxia*

Archaeology generally considers the Neolithic as the era in which civilization was first formed. In comparison with the Middle Eastern civilizations of Mesopotamia—the Sumerian and Babylonian—and with Egyptian civilization, the formation of Chinese civilization that had its own material culture and technologies, while not all that early, has nonetheless been shown by current excavations to have developed independently.[1] This independence does not preclude some techniques and agricultural products as being of Middle Eastern origin.[2] By the mid-Neolithic period, agriculture had already begun in the Central Plain, but this was one element in a diverse economy of farming, herding, and fishing. Since the standards of agriculture at that time were not high, and natural resources vastly exceeded the needs of the population, the lifestyle of the people was a mixture of following a natural way of living combined with the accoutrements of social organization. According to the research undertaken by Yuan Jing, excavated animal bones show a shift in the consumption of meat in the mid- and later Neolithic periods from fishing to domesticated livestock, indicating a turn from a natural way of life to a contrived order directed through human activity.[3] At that time, handcraft techniques of the ancient Central Plain were such as to permit the creation of pottery and implements of jadeite.[4] During the late Neolithic, woven materials and bronzes appeared and, in particular, large concentrations of human dwellings, namely townships, emerged. Taosi in the basin of the Linfen river in southern Shanxi has a large township that covers an area of 2,800,000 m^2.[5] Such a large settlement has led to its being called a royal township. It dates from before the Xia dynasty and may belong to one of the legendary sage kings, probably being about the time of Yao. Moreover, in this location markings have been found that would seem to constitute an early script.[6] Moreover, there are scholars who hold that the earliest Chinese Taosi culture was not wholly that of the Central Plain, but a more hybridic culture. Su Bingqi believes that "while Taosi culture is a culture of the Central Plain, it is not entirely so." Rather, it may very possibly be a mix of Yangshao culture and the Hongshan culture of the Yanshan area. Because the style of pottery and decorations of Taosi culture "include northern elements," the culture has been described as "sparks sent flying from a collision between two major cultural systems in the bend of the Fen river."[7] Clearly, even in the remote past, China was an entity formed out of mixed cultures; it was never a monolithic civilization. This fact may be related to the open nature of the geography of the Central Plain, and perhaps due to other unknown reasons.

Elsewhere, Zhang Guangzhi notes that by the late Neolithic period, the Central Plain already had some of the basic characteristics of Chinese culture. He believes that by that time, there was already the planting of millet, paddy fields, and sorghum; the rearing of pigs, dogs, oxen, sheep, and horses; rammed earth buildings; and also silk and hemp, pottery, bronze, wood carving, and *taotie* decoration; oracle bone inscriptions and hieroglyphic writing. These features probably defined early Chinese culture as it was centered on the Yellow River basin.[8] In addition, excavated objects from places such as Yangshao, Daxi, and Hongshan show that the form of the dragon was present from Mongolia, through the Central Plain, to the Yangtze River basin. The jadeite dragon from Mongolia's Hongshan (Chifeng) is currently the earliest discovered so far, but according to Xu Hong's studies, it is the green turquoise dragon artifact from Erlitou that is the real Chinese dragon, "clearly having its details."[9] These finds suggest that over such a broad area there was already intercommunication among cultures on a massive scale.[10] Zhang Guangzhi estimates that from around 4,000 BC, the cultures of north and south China were "already interlocked to form a larger sphere of interaction of cultures."[11] This was a preparatory condition that anticipated the shaping of a large-scale political system.

According to legend, China's dynastic history began around 2,000 BC, yet for a long time, evidence of the first dynasty, the Xia, has been lacking, and many question marks still hover over it even now. The Erlitou finds in the Luoyang plain that were first unearthed in 1960 are considered by some scholars to testify to the existence of a Xia culture—the carbon 14 tests give a time from 1,900 to 1,500 BC, precisely the time legends ascribe to the Xia.[12] However, other archaeologists believe Erlitou to be early Shang or sometime around the transition from Xia to Shang. Given the lack of definitive evidence, the issue cannot yet be decided. In addition, even if new material in the future can prove the existence of a Xia culture, whether it can also confirm the existence of an actual Xia dynasty may require further evidence.[13] Since ancient times, the Luoyang basin has been considered the center of *tianxia*. If we include the Xia, Shang, and Zhou, half of China's dynasties founded their capitals in this region. In 1963, a *hezun* bronze was unearthed in Shaanxi with an inscription recording the command of King Cheng of the Zhou to found the eastern capital. The text contained the phrase "I dwell in this Middle Country," which is the earliest known written evidence for the expression "China" denoted as "the Middle Country" (*zhongguo* 中国). The "China" mentioned on the *hezun* bronze is the Luoyang basin where the Erlitou ruins have been recovered.[14] Before Erlitou, Luoyang and its surrounding area as the site of the Yangshao and Longshan cultures was taken as the location of the core culture of the Central Plain during the Neolithic era, and there must be some cultural continuity. In Xu Hong's view, Erlitou is the most probable candidate for the original form of China, the first "China."[15] One important piece of evidence is that in the central area of Erlitou are the foundations of a large-scale building that looks like a palace. It covers 100,000m² and the central hall itself is up to 10,000m² in area. At one glance, one can see similarities with the Forbidden City.

The abundance of the Erlitou relics prove that the Erlitou political authorities—it is not important here whether this was a late Xia government or an early Shang government—already controlled a large number of resources and technologies. It was a diverse economy with agriculture as the mainstay, and herding and fishing as secondary.[16] Jadeite, pottery, bronzes, silk and woven goods, wine vessels for both ritual and daily use are common. There were even already two-wheeled carts. Many seashells in the finds would seem to imply that the Central Plain and distant seas were already linked.[17] The direct distance between Erlitou and the nearest seacoast is around 600km. That is not so far, yet Xu Hong notes that the seashells found at Erlitou are *monetaria moneta*, commonly called money cowries, that are found only in tropical seas; hence, they cannot be from the nearer Yellow Sea or East Sea. It would seem they do not originate in the South China Sea either, because "if they were imported from the South China Sea, one would expect to see traces of them all over southeast China, and yet they have left no archaeological traces at all. Hence such a hypothesis is not logical."[18] It seems that the shells of Erlitou came from the far distant Indian Ocean, having crossed the Eurasian steppes and been brought by the northern nomadic herders. Having traveled such vast distances, they were considered as having great value. The mysterious origin of the seashells would indicate that early humans found it much easier to cross vast distances by land than much shorter distances by sea. This also suggests that even during the dawn of humankind, the distances covered in communication and exchange were much greater than we imagine today.

The most significant, and also the most contentious issue involving Erlitou culture is whether the marks etched on its pottery are an early form of script. They do, indeed, look very much like writing, but to date they remain indecipherable. One possibility for this uncertainty is that, as yet, the number of examples discovered is minimal and thus insufficient for them to meet the conditions necessary for interpretation. However, it could also be that the marks are just marks and do not constitute a systematic body of symbols for writing. Yet, such Neolithic marks may be, in part, the origin of the later characters, because structurally there are similarities. Xu Hong believes that the marks of Erlitou are deeply related to the later oracle bone script and bronze inscriptions, but the answer of whether there was a sufficiently mature writing system must await the discovery of "written texts."[19] Zhang Guangzhi believes that these marks are "incidental findings" that probably have not yet been formed into a system of writing.[20] But the problem is that, some hundreds of years later, in the later Shang and Zhou culture, there was a mature system of writing already in existence, with the oracle bone and bronze inscriptions as proof. Moreover, ancient books record, "The pioneers of Yin had bamboo scrolls and edicts inscribed on bronzes."[21] This testifies that the script of the Yin (also called the Shang) dynasty was already sufficiently mature to be used to clearly record organizational norms and describe events. When archaeologists take into account that a script requires a sufficiently long process to attain maturity, they surmise that "we cannot but suppose that the Xia dynasty had begun to use writing."[22] According to Chen Mengjia, the emergence of Chinese characters happened "some 3,500 years ago, and not earlier than 4,000 years," and thus must be "a cultural product of the Shang people."[23] This view is probably not wrong, even if it may at some point need to be revised. If we say it is difficult to predict when Chinese characters first emerged, yet we know they were already mature by the Shang dynasty, then Chen's speculations are perhaps accurate. This question is of the utmost importance because, as noted earlier, a key resource for "stag hunting" for *tianxia* on the Central Plain was the existence of a mature form of writing from which developed a spiritual world with a vast political apparatus attached. From the time that Chinese characters became a mature system, we can infer at roughly what juncture China developed the conditions for a highly rich spiritual world, and this again would be helpful in determining the earliest possible date for the Chinese whirlpool.

From our current materials, we can deduce that Erlitou had not yet become the core of the Chinese whirlpool but had already assumed a trajectory taking it in that direction. Therefore, we can say that Erlitou was early China. Erlitou culture already had certain of the most fundamental genes of the Central Plain culture. Although it is hard to unravel the gene map of the early Central Plain culture, yet we can select certain genes as examples. The palace at Erlitou provides an early sketch of the idea of the central axis that will continue for several millennia afterward. As Xu Hong says, it was China's earliest "Forbidden City."[24] The idea of a central axis runs through the layout of most planned spaces in China, from houses, courtyards, palaces, to cities, even extending to how the state and *tianxia* were conceived. Rooms organized along a central axis constitute a house that is a microcosm of the state, and at another level, the smallest model of *tianxia*. The theological significance of the arrangement along a central axis comes from the metaphor of the center of the earth. The reason why the center of the earth is sacred ground is because its exact center is best suited to supporting heaven. From this one can extrapolate to say that the arrangement along a central axis carries the significance of venerating heaven.

How can we confirm that the theological significance of the arrangement along a central axis comes from the metaphor of the center of the earth? This might seem to be just some arbitrary interpretation that has some mythological origin, and it may not stand up to reason. Appealing to today's scientific outlook that eschews such magical views, the earth is a globe surrounded by the sky and each and every place can be construed as the center of the earth. But if we take a view from ordinary life, the only places we can select as the center of the earth are those that match up with the requirements for life. For instance, such places provide humankind with an appropriate climate, temperature, rainfall, proportionate cycles of day and night, positive *fengshui*, and good topography. Naturally, there is no absolute standard for what constitutes adequate living conditions. The ancient people of the Central Plain measured the shadow cast by the sun via a gnomon and determined direction as noted in the *Rites of Zhou*: "Use a gnomon on the earth to measure the depth of the earth, and the shadow at noon to find the center of the earth. When the sun is in the south, the shadow is short and it is warmer; when the sun is in the north, the shadow is long and it is colder. When the sun is in the east, the shadow declines and it is windy; when the sun is in the west, the shadow increases and it is rainy. At noon on the summer solstice the shadow is one foot five inches. This is called the center of the earth and is where heaven and earth join together and the four seasons interlock, wind and rain combine, *yin* and *yang* harmonize, and all things find rest. It is here that the royal state (China) is established."[25] On the surface, the reasoning here would seem to be that it is because the shadow cast by a gnomon at the summer solstice is "appropriately one foot five inches," but the legitimacy of this measurement is merely a matter of mythology. The real reason is that the shadow cast at the summer solstice being one foot five inches indicates that, at that location, the four seasons can be clearly demarcated, rainfall is balanced, and heat and cold are in proper measure. In other words, it is the best region for agricultural production. And such a place then, is the Central Plain. Evidently, the reason for choosing the center of the earth is in fact that it is a good place, suitable for living. But this reason has been turned upside down to become a myth that establishes what is correct. This myth gives rise to the theological notions of the center of the earth, the four compass points, six directions, and *tianxia*. The Zhou dynasty established the *tianxia* system, and according to the structural requirements of the system, the center of the earth had to be at the center. The Duke of Zhou affirmed the political suitability of his new capital at Luoyi (Luoyang), saying, "This is the center of the world (*tianxia*) that is at equal distance for bringing tribute from all four quarters."[26] The center of the world (*tianxia*) was at roughly equal distance from the four directions, implying that all political relations were likewise roughly on a par. Such a claim is meaningful in terms of political theology, and it also provides a symbol of a political aesthetic, but even more importantly, it gives real facility to political governance.

In addition, the structure of the buildings at Erlitou is an early version of the basic form that will become the traditional design of Chinese buildings for millennia. According to the summary provided by Liang Sicheng, the Chinese-style column and beam architecture has unique external contours. "The roof extends out like wings" above, while below "there are very thick supporting pillars."[27] All buildings are designed with both practical and technical issues in mind, including keeping in warmth, ensuring circulation of air, providing sufficient light, and being able to accommodate stress, along with achieving an aesthetic standard. In addition, the traditional style of Chinese architecture has a remarkable metaphysical intuition behind it, just as the churches and temples of various religions have their theological meaning. That is, the wings that extend out from the roof on all four sides symbolize heaven while the thick pillars symbolize earth. When people are inhabiting their dwellings, it is as if they are living between heaven and earth, satisfying the relational structure that includes heaven–earth–human beings. Chinese thought is, on the one hand, a kind of naturalism, on the other, a humanism. Although there are two sides to this principle, yet they go together. You follow heaven and do what is good for humans. You venerate heaven and respect human beings, diverting from neither the way of heaven nor the path of humankind. Only in this way can perfection be attained. From the human point of view, heaven and earth form the largest of all buildings, while the human dwelling is a microcosm of heaven and earth. Since your residence bears the meaning of heaven and earth, you too ought to follow the principle of being a match with heaven.

The culture of the Central Plain did not establish a transcendental religion beyond humankind, but it did have the theological import of human beings dwelling within nature. Nature is the ultimate standard for the way of all things, and the way of nature is its own standard. As *Daodejing* says, "The way functions of its own accord." The self-referential nature of the way as a standard is the characteristic by which sacred existence is to be measured. Therefore, nature is a theological concept for China. Given that humankind resides within nature, we should follow the same way as nature and be one with nature. Being a match with heaven is the ontological principle for assessing humankind in the world. At the same time, it is a theological norm. To replicate heaven and earth in the shape of the human dwelling is a symbolic representation of being a match with heaven and has a ritual aspect in venerating heaven. Hence, the Chinese abode is not only the sociological idea of a house or home, it is also rooted in a concept of a natural theology. Heaven and earth are unlimited and contain all things, so the human dwelling that takes them as its standard also replicates their inclusive accommodation of all things. At the same time, heaven and earth are understood as households of different scale and construction. The smallest scale of the household is formed by kinship relationships, the larger scale is the collective body of the state, while the household for all peoples is *tianxia*. This common structure that replicates heaven and earth also replicates the theological nature of heaven and earth. As a result, heaven and earth are sacred, the state is sacred, and the family is sacred. In this manner, the way of *tianxia*, the state, and the family can match with the way of heaven. The bidirectionality of *tianxia* to the state and to the family, and the family to the state to *tianxia*, forms a circle that, when taken one step further, constitutes the intrinsic theological nature of the concept of China and carries with it the meaning of its political theology as well.

A sense of religiousness and of divinity is a natural feeling found virtually without exception among all human societies. A sense of religiousness comes from a theological belief that is free from doubt and that often serves as a stabilizing basis for a culture. Hence it is difficult to imagine that any stable, continuing culture could be without a sense of religiousness, although this sensibility need not necessarily be expressed as an organized religion with doctrinal rules, and still less so need it be a monotheistic religion. The key point about a religiousness lies in its sacredness. The form of sacredness easiest to understand is a transcendentalism, namely, some entity that is absolute and external by nature. Hence, most religions presuppose a supreme transcendent being. As a way of thinking, this is the simplest and most effective hypothesis. What is a source of perplexity is why the native culture of China, which has existed continuously in a stable form, has not produced its own transcendental religion. Scholars keep trying to explain this rather baffling fact. For instance, there are the views that morality does the work of religion (Liang Shuming), and that aesthetic education does the work of religion (Cai Yuanpei). Morality and literature do indeed hold a high place in Chinese culture, but they are not what is supremely religious and sacred. Unlike the way of nature, there is no way that morality and literature can take itself self-referentially as an absolute standard. In other words, falling short of the sacred and lacking a standard of constant value, both morality and aesthetics are open to debate and really cannot take the place of religion. For the ancient Chinese, the truly sacred concept was, first of all, the way of nature, and, second, what came closest to that way of nature, namely *tianxia*. After that we have to put "China" that symbolically replicates the order of heaven and earth, and again their sacredness. This is a much more complicated and profound theology in terms of the structure of thought. If we say that the moral beliefs of ancient China were imbued with theological meaning, this is because the way of humankind was understood as conforming to the way of heaven. Nature is where the sacred lies; morality is but a reflection of natural sacredness. Likewise, literature bears witness to the way of nature. The real meaning of praising the sun and the moon, rivers and mountains, plants and trees lies not in the aesthetic effect of the scenery but in the sacredness of nature, or in the sacredness borne by life, the home and state, and the ancestral land.

The theological and sacred nature of the concept "China" may be the deepest reason why the concept of "the kingdom in the middle" has been called into question. If the concept "China" only referenced a central position in the world in geographical terms, then it would be a subjective judgment found regularly in many places and among many countries, where no such opinions should be taken seriously. When some little barbarian kingdom takes to boasting in this way, how much more so the great and powerful? Yet it is precisely because the concept of China has a sacred significance, over and above its geographical appearance, and has the sacred meaning of being a match with heaven, that it does become a heretical concept that stands as a serious opponent of monotheism. Contemporary Confucianism believes that morality is what makes Chinese culture fundamentally different from other cultures. But unlike the way in which Confucianism sees itself, the fact is that Confucian morality is not seen by other cultures as being some special kind of ethics that differentiates Confucianism from them. This was precisely Matteo Ricci's experience of China in the late Ming. For him Confucian morality and Christian morality were more or less the same thing. He thus believed that China was an opportune place for preaching Christianity, and he was unrelenting in his efforts. The difficulties that the missionaries were to encounter later on basically had nothing to do with morality but came from serious differences in ways of thinking and religious attitudes. The Chinese "believers" in Christianity continued to believe in Confucianism, Buddhism, Daoism, their ancestors, the god of wealth, and all of their other gods as well. The missionaries found it difficult to accept this "lack of sincerity." In fact, since the basic questions of the human experience are much the same, the morality of one place does not differ much from that of another. Hence, ethics cannot spell out what is distinctive about China. The unique characteristics of the culture itself probably have a greater relevance than its way of thinking or its particular beliefs.

The "theologization" of the concept of China underwent a process of evolution. For the ancient Chinese, China lay at the center of the world (*tianxia*). This phenomenon may have arisen from a geographical sense. As I have previously laid out, the earliest China was on the Luoyang plain. And not long thereafter, it expanded to Xi'an and then spread south across the Luoyang area to cover what would later be called the Central Plain. This area extended in all directions and thus gave the sense of being a geographic center. While the concept of China from the beginning borrowed the spatial structure of heaven and earth to constitute a natural sacredness, yet during the Xia and Shang it had not yet become a concept of political theology. The Zhou dynasty established a worldwide *tianxia* system that included a great many states, among which China stood at the center and was the patriarchal state. At each level of the *tianxia* system, there was an isomorphism that thus guaranteed the universal transmission of the sacred *tianxia* system within the political order, allowing China to become the core of the sacred *tianxia*. Although the Qin and Han saw the weakening of *tianxia* to become only China, yet China inherited the *tianxia* gene to become a nation with an internal world structure, and carrying this kind of *tianxia* gene made it a concept of natural theology that replicated the order of heaven and earth, and a concept of political theology that replicated the *tianxia* order.

The change in China's physical area also brought about an evolution in its understanding of that area. The original meaning of the term *guo* 国 (state) is a walled town. The original character itself depicts weapons being used to protect a place surrounded by walls. The area covered by a state includes not only a walled town but also its "suburbs" and "wilderness." The area surrounding the walls is the suburbs, including several small towns and the "countryside" (*xiang* 乡). The people who live there have political rights and duties as citizens. The wilds are the large agricultural lands beyond, in which civilized or barbarian peoples live who have no political rights.[28] China was the capital city of the *tianxia* patriarchal state, the capital of the royal house. When King

Cheng of Zhou established a new capital, he said, "I place my house in the central state (China)." This was at Luoyang. Later the idea of China expanded from the capital of the patriarchal state to the whole patriarchal state (the royal domain), and this expansion continued until, by sometime in the Spring and Autumn period, "China'" was used to refer to the Central Plain. In the Zhou *tianxia* system, the many feudal states that had ties of kinship and ritual-cultural links to the dynasty were all within China, including the present-day Yellow River valley areas, such as Henan, Shaanxi, Shanxi, Shandong, and Hebei, that were differentiated from the Rong and Di barbarian cultural areas of the south and the northern deserts. This would suggest that in addition to the geographical meaning of China, there was added a cultural meaning. Once the cultures of the Man, Yi, and the vassal states in the Yangtze River valley (the states of Jing, Chu, Wu, and Yue) had become more similar to that of the Central Plain, and they had attained sufficient power to enter into the contest for rulership over the Central Plain, the notion of China expanded to include the Yangtze River valley. Likewise, as more areas entered into the "stag-hunting" game of the Central Plain, the idea of China continued to expand, extending to an area much greater than that of China today. Its greatest expanse was attained during the Yuan dynasty. In the west, it crossed the Pamir Mountains; in the east, it reached the Sea of Japan; in the north, it included Siberia; and in the south, it reached the Southern Sea. The second greatest expanse and a long period of stability was the Qing dynasty. The western, eastern, and southern extremes were as the preceding, but the northern area included Mongolia and a small part of Siberia. The idea of China itself is a stable and unchanging center while its expanding compass is determined by the whirlpool effect of the "stag hunt" for *tianxia*. In other words, the expanse of China is determined by the number of players who join in the "stag-hunting" whirlpool.

The effect of those entering into the "stag-hunting" whirlpool has made China into a syncretic culture. The manner in which China's syncretic culture has been formed is called "transformation" (*hua* 化). This mode of change is the outcome of both harmonizing (*he* 和) and unification (*he* 合). Moreover, such transformation does not mean that only one side will change unilaterally, but that there will be multilateral changes on all sides. Thus, "transformation" is to be differentiated from religious conversion. It is the cooperative reconstruction by many different cultures within an order in which all coexist. Perhaps the closest mode of change that approaches "transformation" is the variation or mutation of a gene. An even more intuitively direct metaphor might be that of connecting through marriage. In this sense, we might say that the meliorative changes included in the idea of China have a biological nature, or in Taleb's terminology an "antifragility" that rejects a conservative adherence to the original state and that is good at adapting.[29] The syncretic culture formed through "transformation" has become a culture rich in a hybridic composition that is enjoyed together. The various cultures within it are seamlessly blended, making it difficult to recover any original form. For example, the common and orthodox pronunciation of the Chinese language has already been shaped by the speech of many peoples and continues to evolve, with the participation of the northern peoples being dominant. Today there is no speech in any place that retains the elegant diction of ancient China, with the pronunciation of today's vernacular *putonghua* in its most recent form including many characteristics of the Manchu language. In addition to speech, there are many other similar examples.[30] Clearly, China's adaptability is related to the belief that nothing lies outside *tianxia*. It is only the principle that nothing lies outside of *tianxia* that can reasonably explain the openness of this cultural genetic exchange. This then is one evident effect of the continuity of the *tianxia* gene in the idea of China.

While the various peoples and cultures intermingled, the culture of the Central Plain was always the most important resource for this intermingling. This is a natural and obvious fact. As was explained earlier, the culture of the Central Plain possessed an organizational structure and a system for knowledge production that was both more mature and more comprehensive than any other culture. Thus, it was a ready-made cultural resource that allowed for the greatest efficiency in running politics and society. This culture naturally became the rational choice for any people that held political leadership in the Central Plain, even though the nomadic peoples who entered the Central Plain generally retained their original culture in part. The complete sinicization practiced by Emperor Xiaowen of the Northern Wei is an extreme counterexample. In most cases, the lack of a highly developed system for knowledge production and organizational structure for society, including a full corpus of books, large numbers of documents, an educational system, a system of scholarship and of bureaucratic governance, meant that it was rational for virtually all newcomers to accept and become participants in this ready-made and highly developed cultural resource on the Central Plain, as well as to become bearers and promoters of this culture. In other words, the nomadic peoples who entered the Central Plain became cocreators of Chinese culture and were not merely accepting of it. For instance, the civil service examination system that is considered one of the great developments of Chinese culture was created by Emperor Wen of the Sui who was of Xianbi ancestry. This system was improved upon and perfected by the Taizong Emperor of the Tang who was likewise of Xianbi descent. The nomadic founders of dynasties who entered the Central Plain as its masters were no less active promoters of Confucian learning than the Han Chinese dynasties. They gave Confucius at least an equal status as that accorded by Han Chinese dynasties. The Han dynasty honored him as a duke, the Tang as a king, the Ming as the first teacher (that is, as a spiritual leader). In comparison, the Xixia (Tangut-Tibetan) pronounced him emperor (the highest possible status); the Yuan (Mongolian) made him king; the Qing (Manchu) acknowledged him as the first teacher. Another example with a long and lasting pedigree is that it was the Yuan dynasty who first made the Cheng-Zhu School of Principle (*lixue* 理学) the orthodox doctrine for the imperial examinations, while the Song dynasty during which this school first emerged never accorded it such a high status.[31] Xu Pingfang has shown that Kublai Khan's Khanbalik (modern Beijing), planned by Liu Bingzhong, was the closest of all Chinese capital cities to the ideal set out in the *Rites of Zhou*. It had the requisite "nine horizontal and nine vertical thoroughfares, with the palace in the front, the market town behind, a temple to ancestors on the left, and to grain and soil on the right." Even the capital cities of the Han and Tang did not match Khanbalik in their scope and rigorous adherence to the norms of the *Rites of Zhou*.[32] From this evolution then, we can see that the place that originally produces a culture does not have a monopoly on the right to interpret that culture. Once a culture has been shared, it becomes a resource common to all. The way in which many peoples shared in the culture of the Central Plain is comparable to the way in which the countries of Europe shared in the culture that came from Greece, Rome, and Jerusalem.

Mutual sharing and transforming of each other is an indisputable historical fact, but who actually leads and dominates this sharing and mutual transformation does give rise to the sensitive question of who represents China's orthodoxy. The sensitivity of this question is really a function of the historical context. In most cases, most competitors who entered the "stag-hunting" whirlpool all became Chinese people.

The land of origin of the competitor was brought into China when they entered the whirlpool of the "stag hunt" on the Central Plain. It was so for the Xiongnu, Xianbi, Toba, Turks, Western Qiang, Khitan, Jurchen (Manchu), and the Mongols. Before the Song dynasty, the victories of the northern competitors who entered the Central Plain were of comparatively short duration. For up to three hundred years in the Song era, the political structure was separated into north and south. The Liao (Khitan) occupied the north of China with a territory larger than that of the Song; Xixia (Tangut-Tibetan) occupied the northwest while the Northern Song held the Central Plain and the south. Once the Jin (Jurchen, later called Manchu) replaced the Liao, they then expanded their territory south to the Huai River, controlling most of China and virtually achieving the status of occupying the ancient Central Plain as the "center of *tianxia.*" Hence, who is justified in claiming to represent the orthodox China becomes an issue.

The Liao and Song faced each other, with the Song weaker from a military point of view to the extent of them sending tribute to Liao in the interests of peace. As a result, the Liao followed the old Chinese tributary system and proudly saw themselves as the orthodox China. Even so, their diplomatic language remained temperate in speaking of their equality with the Song in the division of the lands. On the one hand, "the territory is divided into two countries," but then "both dynasties form one family"—such language is found in the letters of the Xingzong and Daozong emperors of the Liao to the Renzong and Songzong emperors of the Song. What is most interesting is that when the Taizong emperor of the Liao overthrew the Later Jin dynasty, he acquired the Ten Thousand Generations seal said to have belonged to the First Emperor of Qin. Transmission of the national seal was considered a sign of orthodoxy. The Xingzong emperor of the Liao once included as a topic in the imperial examination: "The holder of the transmitted national seal is the recipient of orthodoxy."[33] Although the Song were weaker, they insisted on their own claim to orthodoxy, basing their evidence against the Liao on the cultural distinction between the Chinese and the barbarians. As Wang Tongling points out, it was precisely because the Song were small and militarily weak in facing the Liao, the Xixia, the Jin, and the Yuan (Mongols) that their "policy of honoring the civilized kingdom and discounting the barbarians became a fixed principle." Research by Ge Zhaoguang shows that the opposition between the Song and the Liao, Jin, and Xixia meant that the Song fell into "a previously unheard-of anxiety about what it meant to be China,"[34] the upshot of which was to emphasize the distinction between the Chinese and the barbarians as a way of justifying the name "China." What is worth noting is that the political narrative of the Song dynasty shrunk from the universality of the mandate of heaven to a particular account, reducing the tradition of the *tianxia* of the world's people to the China of the Han Chinese. This already contravened the universal concern of the tradition of the mandate of heaven inaugurated by the Zhou dynasty and interpreted this mandate as the private possession of one people. Although this impoverished narrative was effective in maintaining solidarity, yet it paid the price of losing the capaciousness and universal scope of the *tianxia* political narrative.

In his *Argument for the Orthodoxy of the Liao, Song, and Jin*, the Yuan scholar Xie Duan employed the notion of division of governance to say that China's political power was divided, with the Liao and Jin being seen as northern dynasties and the Southern Song as a southern dynasty.[35] The division between northern and southern dynasties is usually seen as a temporary phenomenon. Thus, while each has its claims, neither affects the root issue. During both the Yuan and Qing dynasties, non-Han Chinese led the whole of China, giving rise to forceful new questions of authenticity. Both dynasties, in different degrees, accepted the culture of the Central Plain and were deeply intermingled with that culture. And yet because the character of both of them went beyond the parameters of the Confucian narrative dating from the Song, there was no other choice than to reinterpret orthodoxy. Of the two, the Yuan had the greatest difficulty. The Yuan applied a program of inequality among peoples with the basic national policy being to bring the position and traditions of the Mongolians to the fore. It was only for the purposes of governing that they partially adopted the institutions and culture of the Central Plain. The number of Mongolians exceeded the Han by one half in the decision-making bodies, and *semu* (Central and West Asian) people were also more numerous than the Han Chinese.[36] The Yuan also set aside the tradition of using the national seal of the First Emperor of Qin. (The original jade disk made by a person named He had long been lost, and the later national seal was purely symbolic.) The seals of the Yuan emperors were made of different materials and fashioned with a different design.[37] This may suggest that the Yuan dynasty sought to inaugurate a new form of political rule, even a form that was historically new, though such novelty was limited to symbols and signs, and did not really change much.

We may ask how we should understand the position of the Yuan dynasty in history. According to Zhang Zhaoyu, this was a "problem never encountered before" that arose only when Zhu Yuanzhang founded the Ming dynasty. Zhu Yuanzhang put forward a twofold justification for their legitimacy. The Mongol emperors conquered virtually the whole world, something that had never happened before. It was clearly the gift of the mandate of heaven, since without it they could not have succeeded. Since the Mongols had been granted the mandate of heaven and ruled over the whole world, it was the will of heaven that they should also rule over China. However, the Mongols proved unsuitable for ruling China in the end, and the mandate of heaven must revert to the central land. It was thus transmitted to him, making him emperor.[38] Therefore, Zhu Yuanzhang inserted the plaque for Kublai Khan in the orthodox line of Chinese emperors in the imperial ancestral temple. His reading of orthodoxy was not entirely new. It simply reversed the narrow reading introduced by the Song distinction between the Chinese and the barbarians and reverted to the broad tradition of the mandate of heaven dating from the Zhou. The political ideas of the Zhou have a much higher status in the Chinese tradition and an authority that supersedes those of the Song Confucians. Hence, there was no difficulty in Zhu's broader interpretation being accepted.

One other thing worth noting is that while those holding the distinction between Chinese and barbarian of the Song-Ming Confucians cited pre-Qin classics as evidence, relying on the broad principle of "rejecting barbarians" expounded by Confucius in the *Spring and Autumn Annals*, yet in fact it ran counter to the Zhou tradition of an all-inclusive *tianxia* and the impartiality of the mandate of heaven. Qu Shigu has pointed out that the distinction between Chinese and barbarian relies on a misreading of Confucius: "Our teacher (= Confucius), when editing the *Spring and Autumn Annals*, set aside the Yi and Di barbarians, meaning thereby that Wu and Chu, being in fact ministers of the Zhou, were the first to usurp the title of king, and as such, he rejected them and would have no truck with them. This does not mean that he rejected any barbarians who were living in undeveloped wastelands"[39] Qu's reading is not only true to the interpretive context, it also conforms to the old meaning of *tianxia* under the Zhou. In fact, before Qu's time, during the Northern Wei, Toba Gui had the same reading: "The meaning of the *Spring and Autumn Annals* is that unity is good. The state names Wu and Chu have long since been proscribed. Exemplary persons spurned them as the dross of false titles." It is evident that the discussion over Chinese and barbarian had a specific historical interpretive context and was not some general principle that Confucius appealed to in explaining the *Spring and Autumn Annals*. If we take Confucius's admiration for the Zhou as normative, then the Yuan dynasty cannot be considered an illegitimate regime. Nevertheless, although the Yuan displayed unprecedented military power, it only achieved minor and disparate successes on the cultural front. When compared overall with the high civilization of the Song, it marked a major decline and can hardly be held to be a period of civilized rule. The Yuan accepted the tradition of the Central Plain of uniting the whole land as its claim to legitimacy—"from the time of the ancient emperors only those who united everything within the four seas could claim legitimacy."[40] Yet if military prowess is the only consideration and no thought is given to civilian rule, then this is only the way of the hegemon that takes force as its standard. It is not the way of the king that is based on virtue. And it further gives rise to the question of winning the minds of the people, where evidence of kingly way is that the minds of the people are won over by it. Again, it reduces evidence for gaining the mandate of heaven to a geographical factor: the unification of the whole territory. In this reduction, the celestial and the human go their separate ways. Politics and morality are uncoupled, and all that remains is a position that is difficult to defend. Xunzi had already pointed out that the root of *tianxia* lies in winning the minds of the people and not in the land.[41]

However, we should note that the earliest meaning of orthodox rule lay in there being one rule and not in its political orthodoxy. As Jao Tsung-i has shown: "The meaning of orthodox rule is derived from that of one rule" as it is first set out in words of Li Si.[42] Yet, from the Song onward, discussion of orthodox rule largely followed the standard set down by Ouyang Xiu. Ouyang Xiu interpreted the profound meaning of the *Spring and Autumn Annals* from the point of view of the *Gongyang Commentary*. Inferring from linking together "making the great living space orthodox" and "ruling over the great unified area," he asserted that "orthodoxy is that by means of which what is unorthodox in the world, is made orthodox," and "unification is that which brings together what is not united in the world."[43] This suggests that "unification" refers to unity within a spatial area while "orthodoxy" refers to public affairs and amounts to a unified rule from winning over the minds of the people. Bringing together the two kinds of unity, unity of all within the four seas and unity by winning over the minds of the people, is the fullest sense of one united rule. However, in practice, it is virtually impossible to ever attain perfect unity in the minds of the people. Any form of organization or political power can only win support from some of the people. The difference lies in scale or degree. Once the way is lost and there is little support from the people, then rule can hardly last long. This then is the natural adjustment of the way of heaven. To be able to attain united rule successfully requires many good things, one of which is the orthodoxy that comes from winning the minds of the people. There-fore, in simply dealing with the orthodoxy of establishing a state, unity of a spatial area is only the first criterion that one has the mandate of heaven. Sima Guang raised objections to a lax use of the term "orthodox rule" a long time ago because many ways of talking about orthodox rule "were simply a matter of subjective opinion and not the common will of the general public." Sima Guang selected the standard of effectiveness from among what were the commonly held standards for determining the orthodoxy of rule. In other words, could an effective social order be established that could guarantee social stability and allow people to live and work in peace? As he explains: "One who is unable to hold the nine dominions in unity may have the name of the Son of Heaven but lacks the substance. Regardless whether Chinese or barbarian, the gentle or rapacious, the great or small, the powerful or weak, at some time or other they make the claim that they are no different from the various kingdoms of old. How dare they claim to be the sole orthodox kingdom and accuse all the others of being usurpers? If orthodoxy is to be judged from what is given from above, then how did the Chen clan get hold of it? Or the Toba? If orthodoxy is to be judged from living in the center of the Xia (China), then the Liu, Shi (Dan), Murong, Fu, Yao, and Helian were all ancient capitals of the five emperors and three kings. If virtue is the test of orthodoxy, then small states might have virtuous kings while great dynasties might have unworthy emperors. Therefore, the theory of orthodoxy throughout history has never worked and has only led to unavoidable conflict." Again, "What I have set out is that the rise and fall of states comes about from the good fortune of the people. . . . I do not claim to know the difference between orthodox and unorthodox but only speak about the reality of effective rule."[44]

As for the Qing, its legitimacy is beyond dispute. Recently, the New Qing historians have been seeking to show that the Manchus who founded the Qing were a foreign state that occupied China by force, but this does not square with the historical record. Before Nurhaci rose up, the northeast where the Manchus lived belonged to the territory of the Ming dynasty and was not a foreign state. Thus, Nurhaci's raising of troops and getting involved in the "stag hunt" for *tianxia* was a matter of revolt not of invasion. The military successes of the Qing were exceptional, and the territory they controlled was much greater than that of the Ming. In ruling China, they largely inherited the Ming organization, though they did improve upon it. In ruling over many peoples and many cultures, there were many innovations made in their governance. The livelihood of the people was by and large good. The first 150 years of Qing rule led to a quality of flourishing rarely seen in history, and thus their orthodoxy should be without question. Yet, during the early years of Qing rule, in the minds of Confucians nostalgic for the Ming, there was a question about the orthodoxy of the Qing rule. In referencing the fall of the Song, Wang Fuzhi was in fact pointing to the fall of the Ming. "When the Song fell, the transmission of *tianxia* handed down from the times of the Yellow Emperor, Yao, and Shun onward was lost."[45] "The loss of *tianxia*" is a phrase that comes from Gu Yanwu who said, "To change the royal family and alter the dynastic title is what is meant by losing a state. When benevolence and justice are utterly blocked and one can only lead animals to eat people and people to eat each other—this then is what is meant by losing *tianxia*."[46] However, the way Wang Fuzhi uses this phrase distorts Gu's meaning. Although Gu pined for the old regime in his heart, he still did not apply the loss of *tianxia* to Qing rule. The example of "benevolence and justice being utterly blocked" was directed at the Jin dynasty, and the Jin were not barbarian but Han Chinese. Wang Fuzhi's reading of the loss of *tianxia* seems to suggest that the cultural tradition of the Central Plain was severed. This, too, does not square with the facts. It is simply a matter of emotion and resentment. The contribution the Qing dynasty made to the culture of the Central Plain should not be questioned. The worldview, understanding of history, and ethical order of the Qing was that of the tradition of the Central Plain. From the Shunzhi emperor onward, the Qing emperors did their utmost to promote the Chinese tradition and they greatly surpassed the Ming emperors in their appreciation of the classics, history, poetry, calligraphy, and ethical writings.

In the matter of orthodoxy of rule, the point of comparison between the Yuan and the Qing worth discussing is that the emperors of both dynasties retained or simultaneously held the title of khan. This point has constantly been used to argue that the two dynasties did not belong to the traditional lineage of Chinese dynasties, and that they were foreign states that conquered China. On this point of dual identity, people today should not try to second-guess the minds of the ancients but instead should seek for the most reasonable explanation on the basis of the rational conduct of historical persons living at that time. To use contemporary theory to reconstruct past facts has little probability of being true to the historical realities. Rather, we should follow the reasoning of the ancients that would optimize their own benefits in inferring their choices. Or, said another way, estimating the behavior of the ancients by seeking what is for them of greatest benefit according to the common rationale of humankind may enable us to get closer to historical truth. After all, human nature and reason have changed little in the course of history. They are the common factors in all human conduct. Now, speculating on their optimal benefits (predominantly political and economic benefits), for the Yuan and Qing to lay aside the line of orthodox rule of China's dynasties, and to take in its stead the status of an invader founding a conquering dynasty, would have given them an identity that would have helped neither the Yuan nor the Qing to rule the whole of China. It is a choice that would not be in the best interests of the Yuan or the Qing and clearly could not be the rational choice of either one of them. Rather it is a fiction foisted on them by people of today.[47] Furthermore, China was originally a creation brought about by combining the strengths of many cultures and peoples. And for virtually half of its history, China was led by northern peoples. (If we include the Sui and Tang as rule by northern peoples then it is for more than half of its history.) Clearly, we cannot exclude half of Chinese history from China. If we take the part of the Han Chinese to take Han leadership as orthodox rule and that of northern peoples as unorthodox, then by the same logic, the northern peoples could simply reverse this judgment.

The rational argument as to why the Yuan and Qing emperors retained dual titles is that they sought the combined support of two traditions in order to control the varying lifestyles and means of production of two large areas. This is surely the most natural and most rational choice they could make. Moreover, that they held both the title of emperor and of khan was not the first time this had happened. Indeed, this tradition began with the founding of the Tang. The territory ruled over by the Taizong Emperor of the Tang extended to the four seas with vast swathes of land, and hence he assumed the titles of Son of Heaven and Khan of Heaven. In a similar way to the example set by the Tang, the Yuan and Qing rulers felt they had created an empire that was unprecedented in scale. They did not divide their realm into two separate states but saw it as one state with two systems—in fact more than two. For both the Yuan and the Qing, the ideas of the mandate of heaven and of united rule of the Central Plain constituted their most beneficial political-theological narrative. It was only by becoming the legitimate inheritors of the great unified China that they could effectively make use of the greatest resources, power, and benefits. Given that to enter into the orthodox line of Chinese rule provided in the highest degree the greatest benefits for both dynasties, it is hard to imagine that either one would reject a political resource and a historical narrative that was so advantageous to themselves. The Qing were clearly aware of this. For instance, under the Ming and before the Manchus had joined in the "stag hunt" on the Central Plain, Nurhaci wrote a letter to the Wanli emperor of the Ming in which he used the idea of *tianxia* to argue that Manchu rule over the Central Plain was legitimate. "Within heaven and earth, from humankind above to insects below, heaven generates and heaven nourishes them all. Is it that only your southern dynasty nourishes them? . . . The heaven that nourishes the myriad living things accepts all and is partial to none. It is not because your southern state is large that it wins favor. . . . To whom the mandate of heaven reverts is the one who holds *tianxia*."[48] Later, in his *Dayi juemi lu* (Records of great justice illuminating obscurity), the later Yongzheng emperor of the Qing expounded a similar argument.[49]

All in all, the idea of China has always been the outcome of the intermingling and collective construct of many peoples and many cultures. It has not been a matter of a total assimilation to the Han alone, nor has it been a matter of exclusion and separation among varying cultures. Rather it is a genetically constructed remaking. Within the Chinese culture as the product of this kind of comingling diversity, it is the spiritual world carried by the conduit of Chinese characters that is the richest and deepest factor, and it is thus that the genes of the Central Plain's culture have always played a leading role. This too is a fact. Even though the northern peoples—especially the Mongols and the Manchus—entered and dominated the Central Plain, the culture of the Central Plain was still the main resource in the blending of culture. The fundamental reason for this is that, because the northern peoples who made their way into the Central Plain found entry into the historical lineage of China to be of optimal benefit, it was inevitable. The political legitimacy of the Qing, as much as that of the Yuan, can be understood within the context of Chinese thought, at least according to the Zhou tradition wherein the state carries the structure of *tianxia*. There is thus no theoretical or practical difficulty in figuring out how ancient China gathered the myriad peoples into one body.

It was only toward the end of the Qing dynasty that China really faced the problem of articulating its own identity. Not only was China not at the center of *tianxia* in geographic terms, it was also not at the center politically, or even in the production of knowledge. If one persisted logically in following the idea of *tianxia* to understand the world, then since the last years of the Qing, China has no longer been the middle kingdom it once was, and it has become merely one of the peripheral feudal states. At the same time, ancient China's narrative of its own self-understanding encountered doubts raised by the outside world. A narrative that came from others has brought with it a different logic in explaining the world order and has thus given rise to problems of contextual displacement and cross-cultural misunderstanding.

A classic example of this is that since the Han dynasty—and especially since Ming-Qing times—the institution of tribute has been seen as a forceful way in which China imposed a hierarchical structure on the world. John Fairbank has called this practice a "tribute system."[50] He interprets the tribute system as "China's world order, a complete body of thought and action," and he observes that "over hundreds and thousands of years China's rulers constantly developed this system so that it would last for ever."[51] However, to understand the institution of tribute as a system is perhaps an overstatement. Although from the Han dynasty onward the Zhou nomenclature of tribute was retained, it no longer signified submission to the power of the ruler. Basically, it retained the name but not the substance, with the name having purely aesthetic and symbolic meaning. Tribute in the Zhou dynasty was of practical value. The feudal princes had a political and economic duty to support the system of *tianxia*. While their tribute did not amount to taxation—being a weaker idea than taxation—yet it was a partial contribution to the cost of maintaining the system of *tianxia*. But from the Han onward, the institution of tribute was purely symbolic. Apart from a minority of subordinate states that had a close relationship with the Chinese dynasties—Korea, Vietnam, and Ryukyu—most countries that gave tribute did not see themselves as having the relationship of belonging to the Chinese dynasties, and at the very most, they only pretended to be submissive in order to seek their own advantage. The Chinese dynasties did not have an oversight relationship with the tributary states, either politically or economically. Hence, in reality tribute from the Han onward was merely an institution for making contact with foreigners and fell far short of being some system or imposed order. In simple terms, there was no system to speak of, and it had no real power. From the Han-Tang to the Ming-Qing, the tributary relationship tended to be a policy of high returns for low investment, with the greater largesse and higher-value presents being offered to the tribute countries. Most of the tributary states used the favorable tribute policy to engage in profitable trading, and they even went so far as to compete with each other in offering their tribute. The tribute trade became such a vast expenditure for China that the Chinese dynasties had no choice but to restrict the frequency and amount of tribute goods offered.[52] From this picture, it can be seen that the surrounding countries understood tribute as something having economic import much more than as something political.

We also have to pay attention to the phenomenon of reverse tribute. Before Emperor Wu of the Han, the Western Han had suffered from long-standing conflict with the Xiongnu. In order to win peace, the Han had to offer many gifts to the Xiongnu. As Li Yunquan has said, this shows that the Han were offering tribute in reverse to the Xiongnu.[53] Reverse tribute offered by the dynasties of the Central Plain to strong competitors was not an exception. The Northern and Southern Song offered such reverse tribute to the Liao and the Jin. This phenomenon of reverse tribute shows that tribute was a common political strategy of the times and not the monopoly of the dynasties of the Central Plain. The common rule was that the stronger received the tribute. We should also note that tribute was not the only policy by which the dynasties of the Central Plain made contact with foreigners. In fact, the twin strategies of tribute and dynastic marriages went hand in hand. Although tribute was the main strategy, dynastic marriage reinforced it. For this reason, one cannot reduce the relationship between the dynasties of the Central Plain and surrounding political authorities to one of tribute alone. Yan Mingshu has shown that the role of dynastic marriage has been manifestly underrated in modern histories of the period. In fact, the strategy of dynastic marriage has been a constant thread from the Shang-Zhou era up to Qing times. It was not just a one-off matter, nor was it always a calculation of power differentials carried out under duress. Rather, it was a long-term strategy in which the dynasties of the Central Plain were sometimes recipients, sometimes the active proponents.[54]

Strictly speaking, the tributary relationship began to have some degree of political significance only with respect to feudatory regimes and ones that followed the Chinese calendar. The former feudal relation meant a fairly close family relationship, and the tributary could be called on to help China when it was faced by a crisis. The latter relies on the Chinese calendar and chronology to standardize time and the seasons. It may also indicate an acknowledgment of allegiance. According to a very imaginative theory by Shao Yiping, the calendar suggests acceptance of a "temporal sovereignty" that differed from a spatial sovereignty.[55] If a tributary state followed the chronology of the Chinese dynasties, this meant that it recognized the Chinese historical narrative as a publicly available history. Although acceptance of temporal sovereignty does not have the same force as spatial sovereignty, it is still an influential form of politics. According to this logic, given that China today and most countries in the world have adopted the Western calendar, should we then take this fact as signifying that we take the West as normative?

Chapter Three

The Game of "Stag Hunting" and the China Temptation

The earliest exposition of the *tianxia* "stag hunt" is found in the *Records of the Historian*, in which it states: "The Qin empire having lost its stag, all of *tianxia* were on the hunt for it."[1] Here the stag stands for supreme power. Why is it the stag that is chosen for this role? It would seem there is no definite opinion. Power is the prey of the political game, and so it is not hard to see why an animal can symbolize power. But there were many kinds of animals hunted on the Central Plain. And quite a number of them were stronger and larger than the stag. When the Central Plain began to flourish, there was a warming period across the whole globe.[2] The climate was temperate and humid, and the plant cover lush and abundant. There were not only oxen, bears, tigers, and leopards, but even elephants and rhinoceroses. Why then should the stag be chosen to represent power? It seems a rather perplexing question. Perhaps deer were the most numerous and thus most important animal for the hunt on the Central Plain at that time,[3] and perhaps for this reason, the stag can represent all hunted quarry. But as an explanation, this seems to be somewhat inadequate. The earliest literary reference to deer is found in the *Book of Odes* (*Shijing: Xiaoya: Lu ming*) in the poem "The Deer Calls": " 'Yo-yo,' cries the deer." The deer described here is a symbol of gentleness and warmth, and seems to have little to do with power. Zhang Guangzhi suggests that since the shoulder blades of deer are found in ancient archaeological sites where they had been used for divination, they may have had a ritual significance. This may be related to the importance it had for the hunt.[4] Yet this too would seem to be

53

insufficient evidence. While it is true that the shoulder blades of deer could be put to ritual use for divination, the ancients preferred to use the shoulder blades of oxen for this purpose, and even more, the cara-pace of turtles. This would seem to suggest that the ritual significance of the shoulder blades of oxen and the carapaces of turtles was greater than that of deer bones.

Perhaps we can ponder this question from another angle. On the Central Plain in the early times, while tigers and elephants would symbolize force, they are quite fierce as animals. As such, they are not purely passive prey for the hunt but are in fact rivals in the contest. It is only animals that can simply be hunted that are suitable as objects of a competitive game of hunting. And among such animals, the deer is the classic animal of the hunt, more elegant than the wild boar, mountain goat, fox, or hare. The stag has a crown of antlers that makes it suitable as a symbol of power. This view is corroborated by a line in the *Book of Changes*: "When the deer is out of sight, it will find its way into the forest. The gentleman, knowing the risk, should give up the chase."[5] This means that because this deer was under the supervision of the forestry officials, it will hide in the thick forest, and the gentleman should not pursue it. This suggests that by that time, stag hunting was a competitive sport already reserved for the king and nobles, and was under the supervision of specially commissioned officials. Maybe it is for this reason that the deer became a symbol of power.

The key to the game of "stag hunting" lies in the temptation it arouses to participate, a temptation that is so strong that it proves to be virtually irresistible. "Stag hunting" on the Central Plain is a competition for political power with the broad expanse of the Central Plain itself being the goal. Many political actors exert their greatest strength in the search to control such vast resources. Some powers are major participants; others are passively drawn into the game owing to their alliances. As was said earlier, the main characteristic of the "stag hunting" game is that it gives rise to the whirlpool effect. Once one is drawn into it, it is difficult to extricate oneself unless one renounces all of one's interests and land (the chips for the game), and withdraws, as did the Xiongnu and Tujue (Turks) when defeated in the competition. Some of the losers merged with the peoples of the Central Plain, others retreated to the frontiers, while some even gave up their ancestral lands and journeyed far away. Therefore, although "stag hunting" on the Central Plain can reap great rewards, it is still a huge risk. Success and failure are decided in a moment, and not by following the actual history of the "stag-hunting" game. Previously, we have already analyzed the logical hypotheses and surveyed the most compelling reasons why the Central Plain became the focal point of the political game. Here we still need to look further at the geographical criteria that would explain the historical context and evolution of the Central Plain becoming the focal point of the game.

Why did the stag hunt take place on the Central Plain? Xu Hong has proposed two explanations that can help us to understand this. The first is Robert L. Carneiro's theory of circumscription. This theory was not originally designed to explain China but was merely a general hypothesis about any early society. Places where conditions are optimal bring together a concentration of resources. People flow in from all around, thereby increasing the density of the population. Residents of the central area become cocooned and are obliged to increase their strength and expand the range of their territory to protect themselves—and to defeat competitors. As a result, the central area becomes densely populated and is highly volatile. Xu Hong believes that the Central Plain in early times may have followed just such a development and thus become the center of competition. Another explanation is provided by Zhao Hui's centralizing theory. This theory was proposed explicitly for the Central Plain. The center of the ancient Central Plain extended outward in all directions and thus became a central point for communication, transport, and information. As a result, the Central Plain garnered the greatest political experience and thus matured more quickly than surrounding areas. The frontier regions, lacking opportunities to learn, were at a competitive disadvantage. Zhao Hui tries to argue that the success of the Central Plain was above all due to its routes of superior communication rather than being due necessarily to any economic advantages.[6] Both of these theories would seem to be able to explain, in part, the historical conditions according to which the Central Plain became the center, yet they are still wanting as sufficient reasons. The natural resources and population of the Yangtze River basin are no less than those of the Yellow River valley. The flourishing of civilization there was no later—at the most, only a little later—than in the Central Plain. Material technology and conditions of transport were not inferior to those of the Central Plain. Why is it that the Yangtze River basin did not become the center? Indeed, up into the Spring and Autumn period, the Central Plain was still seen as a barbarian territory. Furthermore, if communications and transportation are the deciding factors, why did the western region not become the center? As a much larger space for transportation, the western region extends much farther in all directions and was a center of logistics and information. To the east, it extends to the Central Plain; to the west, it links to central Asia and the Middle East. It has the natural conditions for material and technological exchange between east and west. In fact, many types of material resources and technology were transported to the western region and entered the Central Plain through the western reaches. Among these resources, those of great importance include the smelting of bronze and iron, the cultivation of wheat, the rearing of sheep, the milking of cows, the making of glass, and the use of the horse chariot. These technologies were most probably discovered in western Asia and brought into the Central Plain, as was jadeite from Xinjiang and Khotan. From the Central Plain, many useful technological innovations were transported to western Asia and Europe along the Silk Road at a time much earlier than when Zhang Sai traveled through the western region. Wang Wei thinks that bronze smelting and the cultivation of wheat entered the Central Plain about 4,500 years ago, and techniques of iron smelting came in no later than the Western Zhou.[7] Yang Boda even believes that three to four thousand years before the Silk Road this transportation route was preceded by the Khotan-Yugu Road.[8] His evidence for this claim is that, at the Yangshao cultural site of Banpo of six thousand years ago, objects made of Khotan jadeite have been found. And in the tomb of King Wu's wife, Hao, over three hundred artifacts of Khotan jadeite have been unearthed that date from more than three thousand years ago.[9] The material resources and technologies that were transported along the later Silk Road are too numerous to be counted. Given how clearly important the western region was in terms of transmission, why is it that its own political status and overall level of technology fell far behind that of the Central Plain and lagged behind the Middle East as well? Was it perhaps because the climate and soil were relatively poor? Or was it for some other reason we do not yet know?

Mancur Olsen's theory of the state might provide a useful resource for a political explanation.[10] To succeed, a state needs to have a robust capacity for collective action. Olsen categorically states that a small group finds it easier to engage in collective action than a larger one because the larger one suffers from the serious phenomenon of people wanting to jump on the bandwagon to the detriment of collective action that then goes awry. Therefore, if it is to overcome this difficulty and be successful, a state as a large collectivity must satisfy at least two specific conditions: (1) it must be able to shape a universally accepted common good, perhaps something like the ideal of the virtuous state in Confucianism; and (2) it needs an institutionalized regimen of incentives and disincentives to be used at will, for instance, the clear distinction between rewards and punishments appealed to by the Legalists. According to both history and myth, most of the core dynasties that arose on the Central Plain had both the tradition of virtuous rule by sage kings and openly fair institutions of reward and punishment. Thus they would seem to conform to Olsen's conditions. However, while Olsen's theory may be able to explain the necessary conditions for successful stag hunters, it is still unable to explain the conditions that were necessary for the Central Plain to become the arena for "stag hunting," or how it continued to be so. Why is it that the Central Plain became the place for "stag hunting," a competitive game in which people could not but participate?

The question we are trying to resolve here is this: What particular resource did the Central Plain have that meant one could not help but compete for it and thus that motivated each player to take the risk of participating in the "stag-hunting" game? We may imagine that there must have been many reasons. History clearly records that the overall indicators of social development in economics and politics, and in culture and transport as well, were such as to draw many powers in succession into this competitive game. However, this is not the cause but the effect, and it belongs to the second half of the story of the Central Plain. The real question lies with the first half of that story. The reason that the Central Plain could become a focal point must, of course, have to do with its material resources. There is also another possible cause, though not a fundamental one. In comparison with other places that have abundant resources, it was relatively easy to attack and occupy the Central Plain, open as it is on all sides. The cost of war was hence relatively low. This rather unglamorous reason may disappoint us, but it might well be a secondary factor in explaining a motive to participate in the stag hunt. Various factors such as economic conditions, transportation, and the low cost of war may increase the participants' willingness to enter into the stag hunt on the Central Plain, yet such factors still fall short of explaining the ineluctability of the game. What we really want to understand is not the accidental conditions of the stag hunt on the Central Plain but rather its continuity over a long period of time—its constancy and endurance. Put more precisely, we need to explain why the stag-hunting game took on the dynamic of a never-ending whirl-pool. What factors sustained the centripetal force of this whirlpool on the Central Plain? What we know is that once the whirlpool was set in motion, the stag hunt on the Central Plain was no longer accidental; it became a necessary game. Given that the origins of this story are in the distant past, they are partly hidden and partly visible.

Before humankind had developed the many forms of technology needed to overcome nature, the world was an entity that could be nei-ther tamed nor fathomed. It was thus that humankind used magic as its access to the mystery of what existed. Shamanism, or divination, was the earliest form of magic. All kinds of magic, including shamanism, provided a technology that human beings required for their livelihood. Alfred Gell distinguishes the technology of production, the technology of reproduction, and the important technology of enchantment, a psychological technology used to govern production and for controlling other people's thoughts. In addition to shamanism, there was art, music, dance, rhetoric, and gift giving.[11] There is no doubt that the best known and most sophisticated form of the technology of enchantment resided in religious and political ideology. Even so, it is writing that is the greatest form of enchantment. The discovery of writing not only spelled a deathblow to shamanism, it also became the basic condition for the possibility of success for many types of highly sophisticated technologies of enchantment.

Writing preserves information about all kinds of things, enabling people to retain such things in a stable form, where even if the things are lost, the information is still available. Therefore, through writing human beings lay hold of the past and laid out the future, converting the temporality that belongs to nature into a historicity that belongs to the human being. This is the creation of history out of time. Writing creates an ideal world that exists in an objective format, a world that can express all that real life is and store it in the form of information. It is thus that writing became an indelible contract for the persistence of all things, or said another way, it became the spiritual index of all things. Hence, when compared with relying upon the method of "cap-turing the soul" to possess the objectivity of the ideological world, to lock that soul into writing, something that can be done at any time, is the greatest form of magic.

By relying on the magic of writing, humankind attains a numinous force. Hence, when Cang Jie created Chinese characters, it is said that the ghosts and spirits wept in the night. This was because through writing, human beings became idealists who no longer needed the spirits to speak to them. At the time before humankind could possess the world in a materialistic form, they could only grasp it in an ideological way. People created and imagined a spiritual world that could explain everything. Life could thus go beyond the confines of any given time or place and exist in some ideal form throughout the entire world in all of its dimensions of time and place. Magic is strength, and hence early human beings were compelled to contend for magic. The event of "stopping communication between earth and heaven" that took place in the remotest of times on the Central Plain was a matter of controlling magic.[12] The sage kings took the shamanic power away from the people, reserved its use for the state, and proclaimed that the king alone could possess the world. Yet, unlike shamanism, writing as the greatest form of magic is naturally disposed to being universally enjoyed and cannot be monopolized by any authority whatsoever. As a result, competition for the spiritual world opened up, and sharing in the magic of writing became a universal activity for survival.

The Central Plain discovered writing before anywhere else and led in the development of a spiritual world based on Chinese characters. This spiritual world, where the fleetest of foot arrived first, not only possessed the right to interpret the world, it also held the right to interpret history. As ideograms, Chinese characters can stand independent of any given spoken language and can be understood separately, thus naturally having a universal capacity to be shared. All peoples can use Chinese characters to the same extent. There is no absolute need to use the Chinese language. Hence, Chinese characters having the advantage of being universally utilized, the spiritual world based on Chinese characters became one that was available to all. The universality of the Chinese characters is described clearly by Liang Shuming:

> Chinese did indeed largely opt for ideographic ciphers, and the characters evolved in their construction. The spoken language and the characters gradually went their separate ways. In the beginning, the characters did not conform to the spoken language, but instead the language changed so that it could absorb the characters. The two languages maintained their relationship and were not far from each other. It is not all that difficult for us today to understand what was written in the past, as if the temporal gap can be closed. The meaning

of a character resides in the shape of the character itself, and so other nations and cultures have no difficulty in reading it. Hence distant places such as Korea, Japan, and Vietnam could all use Chinese characters and read the Chinese classics fluently. The result of this phenomenon was to overcome the divisions among peoples and to breach the limits of language. Over time it all came together, and thousands and millions of people, from east and west, south and north, were brought together as one and shared one common historical memory. None but saw themselves as children of the Yellow Emperor.[13]

However, we must remember that the Yellow Emperor came from one of the northern nomadic tribes that later became a core population of the Central Plain. This point must be explored further.

Since Chinese characters were the starting point of the process whereby time was converted into history, they occupy both the beginning of Chinese history and the road it traveled. They became the instrument that shaped the path of the spiritual world. Participation in this spiritual world amounted to sharing in both the embarkation point and the road of history. As more and more people joined in, it meant that they could acquire ever greater political reach and influence to the extent that they were sharing in what was, for their own existence and development, the world that offered the optimal possibilities for benefit and advantage. It is in this sense that the concrete conditions of the Central Plain, and its indispensable, favorable resources, became the spiritual world and a system for the production of knowledge afforded by Chinese characters. This intangible means was both more evident and more important than being a geographical center or owning some material resource. It had the strength of unlimited potential rather than being a means of limited consumption. There can be no doubt that the whirlpool model of "stag hunting" on the Central Plain was shaped by a conjunction of many causes, and yet the most decisive factor among them all was most probably the laying hold of the creative leadership of the spiritual world on the Central Plain, and gaining the right to share in its system of knowledge. Especially important here was the right to the use of precedence, or in other words, to have a firm grasp on the right to interpret the end product of the production of knowledge and to thus claim the authority of history.

The reason behind this decisive cause lies in an obvious political fact. Seen from the bottom up, the reason is one of survival. Once one possesses the power to manage the spiritual world, then one has the right to ascribe names to everything, to define and interpret the world. At the same time, one has the power to establish and explain all norms, laws, institutions, and procedures, that is, the right to legislate institutionally. From this follows the right to define and decree right and wrong, to set the norms for knowledge and to determine aesthetic standards, that is, the right to legislate in spiritual matters. Therefore, by possessing the spiritual world that was in public use, one had the strength to organize the minds and hearts of most of the people—indeed, sometimes all of them. In other words, once one controls the spiritual world held in common by all peoples, one has the authority to determine legitimacy and power over social mobilization. As it states in the *Book of Changes*, "Social mobilization comes from a rhetorical use of language."[14] If, among all possible spiritual worlds that could be chosen, there was one that offers an unparalleled spiritual productivity and the right to interpret history, then it would necessarily become the greatest resource over which the various powers would contend. It would become the place everyone had to win. In early China, when the neighbors on all sides contended for power, the Central Plain in terms of economic strength and military might did not necessarily always come down on the winning side. And even when it did, such strength was not sufficient to be decisive in winning the victory. It was the spiritual world established by the Chinese characters that was, at the time, its best asset, unrivaled and irreplaceable. It was not only its most advantageous political resource, it was also the resource most conducive to survival. Therefore, the Central Plain was destined to become the inevitable place of contention in the game for *tianxia*, with economic, geographic, logistical, and other factors being both a facility and a temptation.

The preceding account is, of course, merely a plausible story based on inference and reasoning. But if this supposition holds, the account laid out as follows will be compelling. The most successful classical example of the advantageous use of power in the contention for the spiritual world of the Central Plain as shown in history should be the Western Zhou political bloc led by the Duke of Zhou. The Zhou people lay to the northwest, bordering the Western Rong. Their state was a minor, border state. After the Zhou had replaced the Yin (or Shang) dynasty in the Central Plain, the Duke of Zhou's bloc used the idea of "virtue" to redefine the reason why the mandate of heaven should revert to them, making it into an all-inclusive universal way of heaven—"only the virtuous are helped"—and replacing the exclusive tribal ancestral god of the Shang.[15] From this transition, we can see that the Zhou dynasty renewed the spiritual world of the Central Plain—making the mandate of heaven "new."[16] This new idea of the Zhou enabled them to inherit the tradition of the Xia and Shang in a creative way, provided them with a claim to legitimacy in the possession of the spiritual world of the Central Plain, and also gave them the right to interpret history. The Duke of Zhou also created the idea of *tianxia*, expanding the political order to its fullest spatial extension and universalizing it in spirit. We might say that the thought of the Duke of Zhou was a revolution in political theology with respect to the concepts of time and space. Time became history; the spatial world became *tianxia*. It was thus for China that a capacious history and a global way of living was opened. It matched the boundless nature of heaven with its unbroken history, and it matched the vast expanse of the earth with its all-inclusive conception of the world. The potential capacity of this spiritual world extended to its utmost limits. And from this we can in important measure explain the early maturity of Chinese culture, and also the reasons why later generations continued this cultural tradition without interruption.

The decline of the Zhou gave other strong powers the opportunity to capture the stag. During the many centuries of the Spring and Autumn and Warring States periods, the foundation was laid for the whirlpool model of the stag hunt on the Central Plain, establishing a stable centripetal force in the "stag-hunting" game. In subsequent history, the succeeding dynasties constantly reinforced the whirlpool effect, increasing its strength and compass. However, as the dynamics of the whirlpool caused China to constantly expand, the center of the whirlpool did not always remain fixed in the Central Plain. In response to the shifting circumstances of the "stag-hunting" game, the center of the game for China was displaced both north and south. When the powers of the northern desert became the strongest contenders in the stag hunt on the Central Plain, and were roughly equal to or exceeded the power of its occupants, then the center of the whirlpool in the "stag-hunting" game moved away from the Central Plain north to You and Yan, and, corresponding to this shift northward, the capital of the Chinese dynasties moved from Xi'an and Luoyang to Beijing. According to Zhou Zhenhe's research on China's cities, the foundation of the capitals of the Jin and the Yuan dynasties gave rise to a new explanation of the center of *tianxia*. The Jin set up their capital in Beijing, naming it the "Central Capital" (*zhongdu* 中都), and thus were the first to explain why Beijing should be considered the core of China, claiming, "The only center of *tianxia* is Yanjing." The Yuan provided a similar explanation for their choice of Beijing: "The Son of Heaven should reside in the center," and therefore it was a matter of "Yan and nowhere else."[17] And yet, however much the center of the whirlpool drifted away from the core region of the Central Plain, the game of "stag hunting" never departed from its spiritual world and always retained the configuration of a whirlpool. On the other hand, from the Song dynasty onward, the area south of the Yangtze River enjoyed a long period of peace and a militarily strategic position, adding to this tranquility its superior natural resources and its stable development of agriculture, industry, and trade. Thus, the economic and cultural center of China moved south of the Yangtze. This shows that the center of the whirlpool in this political game was not necessarily the same thing as the economic center.

The ups and downs of the players in the "stag hunt" as both attackers and defenders were quite obviously closely related to their economic conditions. Within the parameters of economic and military strength, the ratio between the maximum expendable assets a contender possessed and the maximum expected return on investment would determine whether to run the risk of prosecuting this military adventure. Whether to attack or defend usually boiled down to who controlled the most advantageous resources that could be had. This may explain why, when the power of the royal dynasties on the Central Plain was so evidently greater than the nomadic peoples of the northwestern steppe, the dynasties did not seek to conquer the grasslands but were content to overawe them. And, in reverse, it also explains why, as soon as the power of the northern desert tribes was clearly superior to that of those occupying the Central Plain, these tribes necessarily moved south and set up their own dynasties. The most advantageous resources being concentrated on the Central Plain was a decisive factor. The *Debates on Salt and Iron* records the debates in the Han court as to whether to wage war against the Xiongnu. The pacifist faction pointed out the secret of why the dynasties of the Central Plain were ill-advised to use force to conquer the nomadic tribes. They argued that "the land of the Xiongnu is vast and broad and their horsemen travel at will, allowing the situation to easily get out of hand.

To use only a small force will not achieve much; to use a large force will cause resentment among the people because of conscription. If military service becomes a burden, then one's strength is drained away; if one uses a lot in provisions, they will run out."[18] And if troops are sent into the grasslands they will be unable to capture the Xiongnu. This faction continued, saying that "the Xiongnu pasture their herds and hold sway over boundless wastelands, where in the north and south, and in east and west, there is no limit. Not even light chariots or swift horses can overtake them."[19] This being the case, they argued, self-defense against aggression was the best form of warfare against the nomadic peoples. "Do not seek the benefits gained from soil and land; better to save our people from disaster."[20]

Looking at it the other way around, the cost for the northern desert peoples in attacking or occupying the Central Plain was much lower while the rewards were much greater. Once they controlled the Central Plain, they not only held sufficient economic guarantees, they also acquired the use of the greatest spiritual and political resources. Research by Li Hongbin shows that it was because the northeastern peoples from ancient times on had an intimate connection with the Central Plain, and had much insight and knowledge of how to best enter and master the Central Plain, that they had the greatest interest in joining the stag hunt.[21] And the facts bear this out. Apart from the one glaring exception of the Mongols, most of the northern tribes who successfully attacked and won control of the Central Plain were from the northeast (the Xianbi, Khitan, and Jurchen [Manchu]).

The rise and fall of the various powers in the game of stag hunting led to a Chinese model of a cycle of division and reunification described as "a long period of unity that must be followed by division; a long period of division that must be followed by reunification." Such division and reunification is also found in European history. The reason for unity is empire, for example, the Roman Empire, while the main cause of division comes from national or religious sects. Europe's interest in division has been much greater than its motivation for unity. One reason for this is that the centripetal force of the spirit of a nation or of a religion had a stronger pull than the recognition of an empire. Since ancient China did not have any monotheism, its various beliefs lacked any forceful demand for monopolization and were thus able to coexist and accommodate each other. Since there was also no nationalism or racism, the various cultures had no incompatibilities that could not be reviewed and reconciled. Although there were naturally produced cultural difference and certain estrangements among peoples, yet in terms of spiritual force, such divisiveness was much weaker than the temptation toward *tianxia*, with the end result being that that acceptance and accommodation were much easier. However, spiritual reasons were only a necessary condition for unity and not a sufficient condition. In the end, it was necessary to aggressively promote collective activity in order to achieve unification. It was the centripetal force of the whirlpool in the game of "stag hunting" that provided the motive force for unification. Once this centripetal force had developed sufficiently to draw players into the whirlpool, they became part of the whirlpool and eventually made a whirlpool of the whole of China. The whirlpool effect was the necessary force that occasioned unification. For each competitor, it was not in division that the greatest good lay. Division was accepted only when the competitor lacked sufficient force and could only adopt a strategy for self-defense, or when the game descended into deadlock and expedient play. It was toward unification that the great force of the whirlpool drew its participants and where the greatest expected benefits for them lay.

The pre-Qin era is the time of *tianxia*, and the *tianxia* system itself is a unity that includes divisions and is thus a model of unity and division as one. From the Qin time on, with the establishment of a united China, the activity of division and unification entered into a cyclical model. Calculating from Qin times, the period in which China has been separated between north and south has been slightly longer than that in which it has been united. Many northern peoples such as the Xiongnu, Xianbi, Tujue (Turks), Khitan, Jurchen (Manchu), and Mongols have divided up China, and the total number of years when this has been the case exceeds more than half of the entire time. This history also includes times, some three hundred years in total, during which these northern people ruled over all of China as the Yuan and Qing dynasties. But it does not include the Sui and Tang when the emperors were of Xianbi descent. As mentioned earlier, one fundamental characteristic of the whirlpool model is its strong attractive force, making it difficult for competitors who lose to wholly withdraw—only a few of them have managed to keep themselves intact. When a competitor loses and refuses to be part of unification, then normally he will be completely excluded from the game and lose all of his advantages, even to the extent of giving up ancestral territory and going into distant exile. Given that in China's whirlpool model there have always been many peoples, it has inevitably led to the multinational, multicultural experience of a shared life lived together. To live together is a common rational choice, since without it the various parties have no peace, a situation that is clearly not in the interest of anyone. The way in which the many peoples and cultures can exist together, and how they can at the same time retain their separateness in their union, has been an issue that any governing royal power has needed to address. In the *tianxia* era before the Qin dynasty, this issue did not arise because the *tianxia* model itself is a union of separate entities in one body. However, in a large, unified state the coordination of different parts to become one became a new question. In this one unified state the question of how the myriad peoples could coexist led China to discover and constantly practice an inclusive form of governance as one state and two systems, or one state and many systems.

Who discovered this one-state-many-systems model? It must be the case that this one-state-many-systems structure draws its origins from the Zhou experience of *tianxia*, though it was not a Zhou discovery. The Zhou system of *tianxia* was tolerant of difference and allowed all to flourish; in its unity it permitted division; the many states formed one body yet each had its own customs. However, the *tianxia* system was not the order of one state but of the world. It was not the one state with many systems, but a world system that included many states and many cultures. Nonetheless, we can affirm that the Zhou idea of *tianxia* was the inspiration for the one-state-many-systems model. From the Qin-Han era onward, Chinese history has virtually always accepted the political legacy of the principle of "not seeking to change the customs" of the Zhou *tianxia* system.[22] In fact, given that the various peoples in their living together were constantly changing each other, it was not a matter of not changing customs, but of not changing them completely.

The Qin dynasty lasted for such a short time it was not able to come to any final resolution on the issue of one state and many systems. Once the Han and the Xiongnu became involved in the game, they opened up the western region and began to face directly the issue of how many different peoples could live together. The Han adopted the Qin system of governance and thus used unified rule in place of the Zhou system of cooperation among the many states. Even so, the unified rule method only addressed the issue of bringing what was the same under their jurisdiction, and it did not tackle the problem of bringing harmony to what was different among the various peoples. The Xiongnu were roughly equal or slightly inferior in military prowess, but they were still hard to pacify for the Han. The Han court sought to use dynastic marriages to bring them into the tributary system, but the Xiongnu and the Han were competitive rivals and certainly not allies. The tribute system was used in such a way that name contravened facts. Nonetheless, since China had used the notion of *tianxia* from Qin-Han times on, Han was a state that incorporated the *tianxia* structure. Therefore, the Han did not look on the Xiongnu as an equal, foreign state, but as a challenger to the overall order. The northern desert region belonged to an area where the Son of Heaven could legitimately travel, and as the philosopher Jia Yi pointed out when referencing the relationship between the Han and the Xiongnu: "Since the Son of Heaven himself undertakes to love his people, how does this same principle of the Son of Heaven reach down to another people?"[23] This clearly indicates that the Xiongnu are people of the Son of Heaven and not those of an alternative state. The new political experience of the Han in fact first arose from its opening up of the west. In the west, there were many small tribes who lacked any kind of unity, with many of them being in conflict with one another, and with the Xiongnu. They too lived along the Silk Road and had hopes of lucrative trade deals with the Han. Thus, these tribes deliberately forged political alliances with the Han and sought protection from them: "The western region reflects on the Han's might and virtue, and is happy to join together with them."[24] Once the sway of the Han extended to the western region, it was faced with the question of cultural difference. Since the commandery and county form of direct rule was not suitable for the allied peoples of the western region, the Han invented an extended form of governance called a protectorate (*duhu*) to provide supervisory governance over an area.[25] The protectorate of the western regions established by the Han was roughly equivalent in status to a commandery, but it was not one. The protector-general had no *taishou* (executive official) only a *duwei* (commandant) or a *xiaowei* (colonel). This indicates that a protector-general was only a temporary post for a military official and not a post for the governing of society. The main role of the protector-general was to serve as a military outpost, to farm and thus support an army garrison, and to supervise the western region. The maximum number of small states overseen by the protector-general in the west was around fifty.[26] Since the protectorate lacked any executive role, we can infer that it did not interfere with the self-governance of the various tribes. It simply upheld the alliance between the western region and the central monarchy. The protector-general was probably China's earliest form of one-state-many-systems. Its loose-rein principle became the basis for the loose-rein prefectures of the Sui and Tang.[27] The time of the Sixteen Kingdoms is when the northern nomadic peoples entered the Central Plain and set up their own government, ruling over the Han Chinese and implementing a system of different rules for barbarian and Han. The state of Han set up by the Xiongnu ruler, Liu Yuan, was the first to inaugurate such divided rule. The person of the emperor provided the leadership for both the barbarians and the Han, and under him were two sets of officials ruling separately over the two groups. The basic organization was one where the barbarians furnished the soldiers and the Han tilled the fields. The barbarian officials led the army while the Han dealt with the economy and society. Thus, the distinction between barbarian and Han was also a division between military and civilian officials, and the state was divided into two populations: that of the army and of society.[28] Although there were two forms of rule, it was not a matter of one-state-two-systems in the political sense. Rather it was more a case of a divided society and two ways of ruling it.

The Tang loose-rein system, however, did show political creativity. To a certain extent it retained the ancient sense of *tianxia*. The territory ruled by the Tang was vast and the different peoples many. Thus, the loose-rein prefecture became the administrative unit for governing areas outside the normal prefectures of the central region. The principle of division involved was one that separated the people rather than the land. It was a mature and vibrant form of one-state-with-many-systems. It is worth noting that the Tang loose-rein prefectural system was one that took the Central Plain as only the political core and eschewed any consciousness of a cultural center. In terms of culture, it was an egalitarian system. Since Emperor Taizong held a dual role as Son of Heaven and as Heavenly Khan, he was the lord of both agricultural and pastoral areas. He himself was proud of this innovation and proclaimed: "Since ancient times, though the emperors and kings could pacify the center, they could not conquer the barbarians. While my talent does not match that of the ancients, my success goes beyond theirs." The Taizong emperor explained this in the following terms:

The reasons why I have been able to accomplish this innovation are five in number:

1. From ancient times, emperors and kings have largely looked askance at those who might surpass them. I have seen the good in others and taken it as if it belonged to me.

2. When people are doing what they can, they cannot succeed in everything. I frequently set aside their shortcomings and take what they do well.

3. Lords of men always promote the worthy and show them much kindness, and likewise demote and get rid of the unworthy. When I see the worthy I respect them, and I treat the unworthy with forbearance; both worthy and unworthy find their place.

4. Lords of men for the most part despise those who are forthright and honest. They secretly punish and openly execute them, and thus honest men decrease in number. Since I ascended the throne, I look on forthright and honest officials as a buttress to the court and have never chastised even one.

5. From of old everyone values the Chinese and looks down on the Yi and the Di, but I alone have loved them all as one. Thus, they all rely on me as their father and mother.

These five things explain why I have achieved today's success.[29]

Even though here Tang Taizong is boasting about himself, what he says is basically true. At the height of the Tang, talented subjects from among all of the peoples served as high officials. The number of barbarians were many in Chang'an, and barbarians and Han did not differentiate among themselves. Barbarian dress and music became both popular and fashionable. Within the loose-rein prefectures of the Tang, each district followed its local customs with each having a large degree of autonomy. This autonomy differed from one to the other. The highest degree of autonomy was when everything conformed in its entirety to the traditional system of the local people. From administrative officials to the subordinate staff, all posts were filled by persons from the local tribe. In these prefectures, the posts of city supervisor, regional inspector, and governor of a protectorate were held as hereditary posts by the leaders of the local people. In the next level of autonomy, the center sent out supervisory officials. In areas with the weakest autonomy, the center dispatched administrative officials who worked in conjunction with local officials.[30] Studies by Tang Qixiang show that the loose-rein prefectural system was infinitely complex, taking shape according to the specific nature of the relationship. In some such prefectures, connections became so close that they were changed into standard prefectures, while there were also cases where standard prefectures became loose-rein ones. Some of the more distant prefectures were loose-rein only in name, since there was no real rule over them, and they functioned more like tributary states.[31]

The Liao had separate governance for the Khitan and the Han. The northern Eunuch Palace Council used Khitan law to rule the Khitan people, while the southern Eunuch Palace Council used Han rule over the Han.[32] This separation of rule for Khitan and Han did not imply social division, nor was it a carryover from the former barbarian-Han division. Rather it simply applied a policy of governance according to the customs of the respective peoples. Most of the highest officials under the Liao were Han, serving in the top-ranking posts of chief minister, commissioner of privy affairs, military commander, historian, provisioning commissioners, and chief generals. Han Derang was one such minister of high estate, rising to be chief minister, with authority over both southern and northern Palace Councils and being granted the title of king of Jin.[33] The Yuan dynasty system, however, was especially complicated. Overall, the Mongolian system was honored. At the same time, Han law was appended to it, and many different systems were operating at the same time. For instance, the law was a composite drawing on Mongolian law, Han law, and Hui-Hui (Islamic) law.[34] The territory ruled by the Yuan dynasty was especially vast. The sociocultural situation of most regions within the empire was a new experience for the rulers. Moreover, the dynasty was unable to form a stable and mature system before it fell into decline, and hence its system of rule had its inconsistencies. Roughly speaking, in terms of its military rule, the Yuan basically retained the traditional customs of each place. The Ming dynasty, by and large, adopted the Tang system of one-state-many-systems, with the border regions retaining the traditional system of each people. The autonomous circumscription system the Yuan had specially devised for the southwestern peoples was further developed into a mature apparatus by the Ming. The Qing retained the Ming system, using heavily Han Chinese governance for the central region, while on the borders a mixed structure involving autonomy and central supervision was put in place. In the details, there were many improvements on the Ming. Generally speaking, China has always had a political structure of many systems combined together. In the era of the pre-Qin *tianxia*, there were many states forming one body; from the Han onward, it was one state with many systems.

The China shaped by the whirlpool model of "stag hunting" was a hybridic body of many cultures and many peoples, with the many cultures influencing each other on the one hand, and also the problems that come with many peoples blending together on the other. Although what actually occurred was a mutual exchange among these cultures as they comingled together as one, yet because the Han people and Han culture was the dominant group, the amalgamation is often described as "Hanicization." This raises a difficult question. The concept of "Han" is itself a complex issue, and it is often spoken of as being the same as the notion "Chinese." "Han people" is a term adopted by modern anthropology, but the problem is that China was never a one nation state. Rather it was a constantly growing, flexible idea whose expansion was determined by the scale of the "stag-hunting" game. Whoever entered into the arena of the whirlpool game and into its diverse peoples were all cocreators of China. The Yellow Emperor and Fiery Emperor were from the western Rong and eastern Yi. The Shang came from the eastern Yi; the Zhou from the mixing of the Xia and the western Rong. The Sui and Tang imperial families were, by blood, largely Xianbi, and even more diversity was introduced by the Yuan (Mongolian) and the Qing (Manchu). What kind of people the earliest occupants of the original Central Plain were, and what stories they had to tell, is something that is at this stage too difficult to determine. The generally accepted standard groups of the Central Plain such as the Xia, Shang, and Zhou were in fact "visitors from outside."[35] The first settlers to occupy the Central Plain as well as the surrounding peoples who later and repeatedly entered the plain—the Xiongnu, Tujue (Turks), Xianbi, Jiang, Tibetan, Khitan, Jurchen (Manchu), Mongol, Miao, and others—were always in a process of becoming the new Central Plain people by intermixing with them. The result of this hybridity is today's Han people. Peoples in ancient China may be distinguished by lifestyle or social customs, or by the distinction between an agricultural and pastoral way of life, but there was no distinction by race or nationality. Chinese people were said to be descendants of the Fiery and Yellow Emperors, the former from an agricultural tribe with the latter coming from a pastoral tribe that "moved around with no fixed abode."[36] During the Xia, Shang, and Zhou eras, some people from the north or northwest lived in the heartland of the Central Plain. Research by Wang Tongling shows that right up until the Spring and Autumn period, there were still a few feudal states of northern or northwestern peoples in the Central Plain, in what is now Shaanxi, Shanxi, Ningxia, Hebei, Shandong, and Henan.[37] Since they had lost in the "stag-hunting" game, they had no other option but to retreat from more naturally fertile areas in the Central Plain to less fertile areas of desert in the north. The last of the strong northern barbarian states to fall was the state of Zhongshan (in the center of what is now Hebei), which was not attacked and defeated by Zhao until the mid–Warring States time. From the Han onward, the northern desert powers regained strength and at various times reentered the "stag-hunting" game. Rather late to enter the Chinese whirlpool were the Turfan Tibetans, while those Tibetans from more developed regions (Qinghai-Gansu) entered the game much earlier and cleaved off portions of the Central Plain many times. In 763, the Turfan attack on Chang'an, the capital of the court on the Central Plain, came as a great surprise. These forces almost conquered the Central Plain but ended up in defeat.

From the whirlpool model, it can be seen that "China" is a concept that goes far beyond that of the "Han." Any subjective account of the concept of China is necessarily going to be biased. Therefore we can only define it from the objective structure of the motive force of the stag-hunting whirlpool, and the hard historical facts of its inclusive pattern of growth. The erstwhile historical facts remembered in history books are frequently the construct of alternative perspectives and of subjective narration. If we take the most complicated case of the Yuan dynasty as an example, we have the Ming dynasty account of the Yuan, the official history compiled by the Yuan, the traditional Mongolian account, and the understanding of the Yuan from the point of view of the western regions. Each one of these accounts is different. They all provide us with subjective "soft" facts. We can only try our best to use hard facts, that is, the account that is most commensurate with what actually happened. Such an account is limited to the facts that, as previously described, can be rationally inferred when we take as the standard the optimal benefits available to the political and economic interests of those involved. They are the facts that appeal to what served the greatest benefits of the historical actors as the objective evidence needed to understand history. From this point of view, while the Yuan dynasty had a great respect for Mongolia, its greatest benefits lay in the Central

Plain. Hence Kublai decided to become emperor of China as the rational choice that offered the optimal degree of benefit. This also explains why after Emperor Shun's troops had been defeated and the emperor retreated to the northern desert, he still saw himself as emperor of the Yuan dynasty, what history now calls the Northern Yuan. Later, because these actors returned to the attack and lost, the Yuan collapsed utterly.

Wang Tongling's *History of the Chinese Nation* uses virtually flawless material to describe the process of the intermingling among and assimilation of the many peoples of China. His discoveries show historical dynasties were established by different peoples: the Jin and Qing were created by the Manchu; the Former Zhao and Later Zhao, Xia, Northern Liang, and Yuan were created by the Mongols; the Former Yan, Later Yan, Western Yan, Southern Yan, Western Qin, Southern Liang, Northern Wei, Northern Zhou, Northern Qi, and Liao were created by mixed Manchu-Mongol peoples (Xianbi, Khitan, and others); the Later Tang, Later Jin, and Later Han were created by the Hui people; the Former Qin, Later Qin, Later Liang, and Xixia were created by Tibetans. Furthermore, among states that proclaimed themselves to be Han Chinese, Qi was in fact a mixture of Han and eastern Yi; Qin was a mixture of Han and western Rong; Jin and Yan were a mixture of Han and northern Di; Da Li was a mixture of Han and Miao; and in the large dynasties of united rule that considered themselves the Han Chinese—the Qin, Han, Jin, Sui, Tang, Song, and Ming—they were a hybridic mix of the many different peoples.[38]

Whether or not the various populations of ancient China had a natural ethnocentrism, the important thing is that outside peoples were not perceived as subject to discrimination or taboo. There were rarely cases of ethnic limits that could not be crossed. In ancient politics, exercising political power was the source of the greatest benefit. That a dynasty should exclude another people from participating in political power would seem to be the most direct evidence for ethnocentrism. Wang Tongling has discovered that whoever ruled China, the political power that was exercised and the ruling class that exercised it, was open to all peoples. He sets out detailed evidence to prove that the leading officials in each dynasty came from many different peoples. For instance, in dynasties with a Han majority, the number of non-Han officials recorded in the historical records—these normally being high officials and famous people—are as follows: in the Sui dynasty there were fifty-one in all, including Xiongnu, Xianbi, and other barbarians.

During the Tang dynasty, there were 122 in all, including Xianbi, Tujue (Turks), Korean, Turfan, Khitan, Uyghur, Japanese, and Indian. Most were famous generals and distinguished ministers such as Yuchi Rong Jingde (also known as Wei Chigong) who was Xianbi; Geshu Han, a Turk; Go Seonji, Korean; Yuanzhi, a Xianbi; Li Keyong, a Shatuo. According to the *Zhenguan zhengyao*, in the early Tang the number of non-Han officials with a rank of five grades or above reached up to one half of the total.[39] In the Song dynasty there were 34 non-Han officials in all, including Xianbi, Xiongnu, Tujue (Turks), Dangxiang, and Arabs, including the famous general Huyanzan who was Xiongnu. During the Ming dynasty there were 174 persons, including Mongols, Jurchen (Manchu), and Uyghur. And the situation was similar in the reverse case when the court was ruled by non-Han leaders. In these cases, the historical records number 68 Han officials under the Liao, including two of high rank, Han Derang and Zhao Yanshou. In the Jin there were 277; in the Yuan there were 37 Han officials of high rank whose merit was such that they were given Mongolian names, including the famous generals Tian Ze, Zhang Rou, and Zhang Hongfan.[40] In the Qing, the number of Han officials exceeded that of Manchu and are names so well known that it is not necessary to list them.

Another standard of evidence for inclusion is that of intermarriage. Throughout history intermarriage has been very common (including marriages between the royal family and other tribes). There was no rule forbidding it. Only during the Song and Yuan was it frowned upon, with the Song being the extreme case: the imperial family never married non-Han persons. The Yuan imperial family rarely married the Han: only nine Han women married into the family and no royal princesses married a Han.[41] From this record it is clear that intermarriage among the peoples was the historical norm, while prohibition of such marriages was the historical abnormality, an accident resulting from an intensification of conflict.

While Han culture itself drew its basic genes from the culture of the ancient Central Plain, it was the result of a constant intermingling among many cultures. Therefore, it would be more correct to call it Chinese culture. If we had to describe what is most characteristic about Chinese culture, then perhaps we could say it is one that has Chinese written characters as its key bearer, that has a spiritual world that is open and welcoming, and that has a core gene but yet is borderless. This spiritual world is always in the process of growing. In history it has already absorbed information from many cultures. In the process of mutual exchange between these many cultures, there have been many changes in organization, dress, the arts, music, food and drink, tools, languages, and customs. Only Chinese characters, as the bearer of this spiritual world, have maintained their extraordinary stability. That is, it is the Chinese characters inheriting and continuing the Chinese culture that is its most basic gene.

The extraordinary stability of Chinese characters may well be related to the hieroglyphic nature of the writing. On the one hand, as a medium for expressing the outside world, the characters establish an objective world. On the other hand, as hieroglyphs, the characters themselves do indeed constitute an imagistic world whose meaning is sufficient in itself. Hieroglyphs not only give form to a conceptualized meaning of what cannot be seen, they also provide it with a visible image that can be seen. They do not simply have significance as abstract concepts, but they also have an added visible (or an aesthetic) aspect and an affective meaning. Thus, they constitute a possible world that contains the whole of life's meaning. It may be said that Chinese characters are not only a medium for the expression of thought, but at the same time a living place with a heart at its center. Because of this, Chinese characters are at once a tool and a world. This special characteristic of hieroglyphic Chinese characters means that they go beyond being mere symbolic signifiers and have an independent meaning of their own. Normally the meaning of the sounds of a language is in the signified or the referent. It can be said that the significance of the linguistic marker is its significance or reference. This implies that the marker itself has no independent meaning. If it loses the defined relationship with what it signifies then it becomes quite empty of meaning, a purely arbitrary mark that cannot be recognized. As hieroglyphs, Chinese characters have a dual significance: the signified meaning and the meaning of "presentment." That is, they can point to an object while, at the same time, they are also themselves something to be viewed. Gongsun Long's obscure statement may be said of the uniqueness of Chinese characters: "When of things, not one is not indicated, then to indicate is to not indicate."[42] Things are all objects indicated by Chinese characters, but the meaning of Chinese characters is not confined to this indicating but goes beyond the meaning of what is indicated. Chinese characters as indicators certainly have the role of marks that refer to something, but these indicators themselves have an independent meaning as hieroglyphs. They construct a "world without things,"[43] an inner spiritual world independent of the objective world. Therefore, Chinese characters thus go beyond the scope of semiology, belonging also to mythology, psychology, and philosophy.

Going one step further, we can say that what is constituted by the hieroglyphs of Chinese characters is not only a spiritual world. At the same time, it is also a spiritual subject that has its own active role, that is, an anonymous subject, a cultural subject. The characters have the function of being both what is thought, the *cogitatum*, and the "I" that thinks, the *cogito*. A Chinese soul living in the world of Chinese characters always has this dual subjectivity: the subjectivity concretized as an individual mind, and the subjectivity of the collectively shared spirit of Chinese characters. Thus, such persons always gaze on the world with this dual subjectivity: a particular mind that looks at the world and simultaneously the spirit of the Chinese characters that also see the world. In other words, they have a dual perspective on the world, from both the "I" and the "we." The classic example is that of ancient poetry that, on the one hand, expresses the external world seen by the poet and, on the other, is the poet's self-sufficient symbolic world constituted by the Chinese characters. This means that poetry has the effect of juxtaposing the natural world and the symbolic world, allowing each to corroborate the other. In one respect Chinese characters indicate things by a symbol; in another they give form to the spirit by symbols. The coming together of the form of the spirit and the form of nature is the point at which "what is above form" and "what is below form" meet.[44] Thus, they bestow particularity and universality, and ensure that history has contemporaneity. The thickness and depth of this phenomenon has without doubt an enduring, spiritual force of attraction.

The "Hanicization" of China is evidently linked to the force of attraction emanating from the spiritual world of Chinese characters. But the reason why this spiritual world became the optimal focal point for all those subject to the forces of the stag hunt is ultimately a matter of rational choice with respect to their own best interests by those who fell into the hunt. By rational choice is meant the quest, first of all, for maximum security, and second, for maximum resources. The hybridic Han people who accepted hybridic Han culture being the majority in China, that other peoples who had the ability to enter the Central Plain, part or whole, claimed Han culture as their own, was manifestly the best strategy by which they could guarantee maximum interest at the least cost to themselves. It was not only beneficial in terms of political security and economic interest, it also meant that they could borrow the spiritual world of Han culture to give themselves political legitimacy. Furthermore, through taking advantage of the long experience in bureaucratic governance, they could maintain political order. Since the spiritual world that is borne by Chinese characters has the greatest space for storage of information and the greatest facility in the generation of information, it thus has the greatest capacity for the input and output of information. In terms of the construction of political theology and the historical narrative, as well as the establishment of social institutions and their organization, Han culture was the optimum resource. For victors in the stag hunt, it was an advantage that was both manifest and evident. One could hardly miss it wherever one looked, unless it was irrationally rejected in a fit of anger. None would refuse to employ this optimum resource to guarantee their own optimal interest. The earliest instance of the self-conscious use of the historical narrative of the Central Plain to serve as a "corrective" for themselves was that of the Toba Wei (Northern Wei). Emperor Xiaowen issued administrative decrees to carry out full-scale sinicization, holding that the Xianbi were collateral descendants of the Xia tribes of the Central Plain to which the Yellow Emperor belonged:

> Of old the Yellow Emperor had twenty-five sons, some of whom were inside and counted as the many kinds of Chinese; some were outside and scattered among the distant subject peoples. The youngest son, Chang Yi, was granted the feudal land of the north. His state had the great Xianbi mountain from which it drew its name. . . . The Yellow Emperor reigned by the virtue of earth. In the north, in popular speech earth (*tu*) is pronounced as *tuo*, and kings are called *ba*, from which the family name Toba was derived.[45]

The Xianbi, Khitan, Jurchen (Manchu), and even the Mongolian Yuan, all without exception, actively accepted the spiritual resources of the Central Plain. Before the Western spiritual world had entered into the eastern half of Asia, the spiritual world borne by Chinese characters was the unrivaled spiritual resource of this vast area, and Chinese culture naturally became the common resource used by all.

For all the many peoples who were stag hunting on the Central Plain, strength or weakness, victory or defeat, were not determined in advance. The only unchangeable thing was the whirlpool model. And the compass of the whirlpool in the stag-hunting game determined the substance of China. Any place that was drawn into the game of "stag hunting" became an interior part of China, while any place that was not affected by the game remained external to China. Since, in the course of history, the substance of China was a constant variable, the idea of inner and outer is one that is easily misread. In the *tianxia* era of the pre-Qin times, and based on the principle that nothing is external to *tianxia*, *tianxia* was boundless. Yet the area ruled by each political authority was bounded. Therefore, in respect of the land ruled by the various political authorities, there was a distinction between inner and outer. In terms of the royal domain of the Zhou ancestral state, all princely states were external and they were each external to one another, while the feudal princely states bound by ties of consanguinity to the royal house (what are called the "Chinese"), the covenanted princely states of the Eastern Yi, Northern Di, Western Rong, and Southern Man, were external. For all the princely states within the *tianxia* system, those in remote areas in all four directions who had not yet entered the system were outside. After the end of the *tianxia* system, the whole Central Plain fell under the direct rule of the Qin—rather like the royal domain of the Zhou kings. Areas contiguous to the Central Plain were external areas that were not yet governed, though they were distinct from the foreign states that had no relationship whatsoever with the central land. After the Qin and Han dynasties, *tianxia* was no longer a political institution but was still a philosophical outlook. Therefore, inner and outer did not refer to China as distinct from foreign countries but was a distinction between areas that were governed and areas that were not. It was a concept of inner and outer distinguished in terms of the boundaries of political authority, and not a matter of boundaries between states. Therefore, inner and outer in China can only be interpreted as a mutable concept: places the Chinese whirlpool reached were internal and places it did not reach were external.

Here we cannot fail to mention what is frequently misread as China's border: the Great Wall.[46] Before the building of the Qin Great Wall, China had already built many such long walls whose remains are still visible. In the Spring and Autumn and Warring States periods, the princes contended to be hegemon, war was frequent, and each state began to build its own great wall to protect itself. These were not border walls but instruments of war built on military grounds according to the topography. Qi was the first state to build a long wall that reached a thousand *li* in its southern section. The southwestern portion of it was a defense against Jin while the middle portion and southeast sections faced off against Chu and Yue.[47] In fact Qi was not territorially contiguous with either Chu or Yue, there being several minor states in between. But, as large states, Chu and Yue regularly crossed boundaries to engage in warfare. The states of Chu, Lu, Wei, Qin, Yan, Zhao, and Zhongshan all began to construct their own long walls. Most of these walls were to defend against or for the purpose of attack on other princely states in the Central Plain, with only a few being used to defend against the pastoral peoples of the northern desert. Qi's long wall was wholly dedicated as a defense against princely states of the Central Plain. Both Yan and Zhao had walls in the north and south, where the northern walls defended against the pastoral peoples of the northern desert while the southern ones faced the states of the Central Plain. The long wall of Zhongshan, ruled by the nomadic White Di, faced west as a defense against Zhao.[48] The wall of Chu faced north and was used to defend against or as a base to attack the Central Plain. Examples are many. Clearly, the construction of the walls of each state depended on the direction from which competitors might come. The Great Wall of Qin, however, was made exclusively as a defense against the pastoral nomads. This was because, after Qin had united China, the only opponents left were the powers of the northern desert, with the western region not yet having been drawn into the "stag-hunting" game. The many long walls that were built subsequent to the Qin era likewise testify to the fact that the significance of such walls depended on the identity of one's competitors. The Great Wall was not the state border between Han Chinese territory and nomadic lands. The Northern Wei dynasty, for example, built a wall in Inner Mongolia to fend off the Rouran, who like the Wei were also a nomadic people.[49] The Goguryeo, centered in north Korea, repaired the Great Wall to ward off attacks by the Tang dynasty.[50] The Liao dynasty built a very long wall from Heilongjiang through Liaoning to Inner Mongolia. The Liao territory included land north of this wall that was not a foreign state, stretching up to part of Russia, and including the whole of the northeast and even part of eastern Siberia. This means that the Liao wall fell wholly within Liao territory, in fact, virtually running through its center. Clearly, it had nothing to do with any state boundary. Rather it was to ward off the ferocious and untamed Jurchen (Manchu), Shiwei, and their ilk.[51]

The real reason why many walls were placed where the Qin and Ming Great Walls lay, or slightly to the north or south of them, was that this was the boundary between ancient China's two major economies: pastoral (including fishing) and agricultural. At the same time it also corresponded roughly to the line between the seasonal climate of eastern China and the dry northwest. It is the line marking off China's 400 mm of rainfall, and the line between semi-humid and semi-desert zones. It corresponds largely to the Hu Huanyong line, a slanted line from Heihe City (Heilongjiang) to Tengchong (Yunnan). This line on the map is obviously not perfectly straight owing to topographic features around which the wall circles or charts a jagged course. Hu Huanyong initially used statistics to determine three maps—a topographical map of China, one of rainfall, and one of population—that all proved to be roughly similar. This line has many overlapping meanings. To a great extent it influenced the state of play in the "stag-hunting" game and divided ancient China into pastoral and agricultural areas of power. It was often the line demarcating the two—or multiple—systems of the one state. However, this boundary is only approximate. Outside the Great Wall there was also agriculture.

Looking back over a long period of time, we find that the military power of these two areas was roughly equal. Each had its periods of expansion and decline. The distinction between the different means of economic production and lifestyle meant that the Great Wall easily became a line marking a balance between the two contestants in the game. When they were exhausted and renounced war, or when they more rationally made peace with each other, they frequently called a halt along the line of the Great Wall. Yet, wherever the balance in the game was disturbed, then land changed hands frequently, as in the Hetao region (Ningxia-Ordos) that, while in the dry zone, nonetheless was well suited to irrigation and thus supported both agriculture and pasture, as was the case for Hetao from the Warring States period onward.[52] Overall, from the time China's "stag-hunting" game moved from being an east-west to a north-south conflict, the area around the Great Wall was the classic line marking the balance in the game, unless one side with overwhelming strength was able to achieve a unified rule.[53] Of course, the Great Wall was not the only line marking a balance in the game. In times of north-south conflict, the north overcame the south more than the other way around. This being the case, in addition to the area of the Great Wall, a second line marking the balance in the game was the area of the Huai River and the Qinling Mountains, with a third area being the Yangtze River. To conclude, the Great Wall was not only not a border, it was the central region of the "stag-hunting" game, the line between north and south in China. This can also explain why the core of China shifted from the Central Plain to Beijing according to shifts in the game's whirlpool. Beijing happened to be close to the line marking the balance in the game and was best placed to control the play of north and south. Therefore, dynasties of unified rule that were able to master both north and south invariably chose to fix their capital at Beijing. Su Bingqi advances an even more positive explanation. He portrays the area of the Great Wall as "the melting-pot of all national cultures," a most lively space in which agricultural and pastoral cultures interchanged. Although there was conflict, yet it was far more a case of mutual accommodation and cooperation.[54] Ever since the Great Qing unified areas north and south of the Great Wall, the wall became a place for reminiscence, a relic of the past.

The point of rise or fall, loss or gain, is where what is comes to naught, where success turns to failure, and where at the turn of the head, all is empty. The whirlpool is an ancient Chinese tale. Contemporary China has already entered into a new type of contemporary game. However, the pattern of China's growth has already shaped a methodology for its long existence. And where there is a method, the mountains are green.

Chapter Four

Method and Destiny

While the Chinese whirlpool may have been brought about by certain historical factors and its evolution can be traced continuously without interruption, yet there are also reasons to understand it as a methodology. As was said earlier, several thousands of years ago, people from all four quarters constantly became involved in the game of "stag hunting." Some of them seized the opportunity and became masters of all; some were able to remain in power for a long time because the people were content with their rule; some took their benefits and blended in; some retreated and came away empty. Dynasties rose and fell; new persons often appeared; time and tide changed frequently. Yet the rise and fall, success and failure of the historical actors only altered the individual episodes of the story, without changing the deep structure of the narrative itself, namely, its whirlpool model. Hence, China never broke apart. Some ancients called this the decree of heaven (*tianming* 天命), as if to say there was some invisible hand behind it. While the decree of heaven cannot be seen, its traces can still be followed. What can be seen in history are human doings, while the decree of heaven is an anonymous method concealed in these human doings. The reason why the decree of heaven is anonymous is because it does not belong to any given actor in the game. Rather it belongs to the method through which the whirlpool was sustained. The leading force over the past three thousand years that has upheld the Chinese whirlpool is a civilization that has "becoming" (*bianzai* 变在) as its existential methodology. The method is the decree of heaven.

"Becoming" eschews any clinging to a fixed substance (*gushoubenzhi* 固守本质). Its root nature is a method, and so it can have implicated in it may different entities. The substance of a thing is its unchanging identity. It is a delimitation that rejects anything different from itself. While a substance that sustains its own identity does not lose its nature, it does not necessarily continue to exist for a long time. An entity that is "becoming" does not draw limits in order to sustain its identity and thus does not eschew substantial changes. It can become involved in everything that is unlike itself and transform otherness into its own nature. So it is that China has been able to exist for a long time. The longevity of spatial China and the reason why it has not been dismembered by external forces draws on the temporality of China's methodology, that is, its method of growth as "being in becoming" (*yibianerzai* 以变而在). The first people of China chose the existential methodology of being in becoming and thus presaged China's destiny. They constantly grew under the losses and gains of deliberate change, and the challenges that change forced upon them. Thus, we can say: The being of China's existence lies in the methodology of its becoming. We might call this the methodology that made China China. The methodology of becoming shaped the Chinese spiritual world in which the classics and history are one, and in which the classics and history reinforce each other. Since history was the classics, history would not stop, and the classics could continue. Since the classics opened the way for history, the classics expounded the way, and history created the reality.

Whatever method is adopted will decide what kind of spiritual world is constructed. If a civilization can construct an irreplaceable spiritual world, then it has a decree from heaven that can never be undone. What do we mean by irreplaceable? Certainly not "incomparable" (or "incommensurate"). What is simply incomparable only makes reference to its individuality. While the individuality of a civilization has its own uniqueness, yet such uniqueness is not the reason why a civilization can exist. Its uniqueness cannot be called upon to explain the existential vitality of a civilization. There is no civilization that can rely on its individuality to exist over a long period of time, and there is no incomparable character that is irreplaceable. Hence, "incomparable" does not amount to "irreplaceable." The reason why a civilization can endure must be because it is able to construct a complete universal narrative system by means of which it can explain the basic questions of life: the world, the future, other people, life and death, rise and fall.

Furthermore, maybe it has a capacity for "robustness" (*qiangjiandenengli* 强健的能力)—this term comes from game theory—and so is immune to all attack.[1] Or it may be that there is a capacity for infinite change that is able to open ever new paths for growth, a capacity that can respond to each and every change. Chinese civilization belongs to the latter. Stated simply, for a civilization to exist for a long time it must have an interpretation of life that produces results over a long period of time. An inability to provide such an explanation would lead to its demise.

No spiritual world has beliefs—whether religious or metaphysical— that are not open to doubt. Now not being open to doubt is not the same as cannot be doubted. Rather it means that while one can doubt such beliefs, such doubting will never lead to some firm conclusion that would make the doubting itself pointless.[2] This kind of spiritual belief is a necessary premise for and limitation on life and thought. Such a belief suggests there is a limit to free will and the power of thought, that is, a limit to subjectivity. The fact that the limit cannot be crossed is precisely what grounds the belief. Beliefs that can work as the limits of thought, whether philosophical concepts or literary symbols, all have a mythological import, though they need not be expressed in mythological accounts. While such mythological beliefs are not necessarily the foundation of knowledge, they are certainly the basis for life. Without its mythology, humankind has nowhere to stand.

On the Chinese mythological horizon, the human being in the world cannot imagine a life without heaven and earth. Since any kind of possible life must develop between heaven and earth, heaven and earth are thus the limits for a possible life, the grounds for a life. It is for this reason that the trigrams for heaven (*qian* 乾) and earth (*kun* 坤) are the root of the images in the *Changes*. Heaven is broad and earth enduring, producing the myriad things and enabling their growth. Hence, heaven and earth comprise the way of all that exists. They are the only model that humankind has to imitate. It is thus that the sage "imitates heaven" and "models earth."[3] The sage seeks to establish ontological affinity with nature and win the protection of heaven and earth. Accordingly, the human way will match that of heaven, and human beings may share in the great virtue of the unceasing life of heaven and earth.[4] This is the basic meaning of respecting the enduring nature of existence.

To divide nature into two as heaven and earth is not only a mythological layout, it is also a philosophical organization. Here, myth is philosophy and philosophy a myth. If existence from beginning to end was purely "one," then existence would be a tautologous definition of itself. If that were so, there would be no change and no meaning. As such, it would not exist in time, being only a pure concept with no actuality. Pure atemporal being is not an actual existent. It is a state that has neither come about nor has any succession. It has no relationship whatsoever to life or living. The temporality of existence can never be defined as an infinite repetition of the same thing; it can only be proved by change. Change is the only evidence for real existence, just as it is the only true measurement for time. Since existence must be realized as change, then at the very least it needs to have two different states in order to form a dynamic between them and generate change. Therefore, the sage used the simplest possible model in taking the two poles of heaven and earth to give expression to the synergy of existence. These poles are also those of yin and yang, and of the trigrams qian and kun. Humankind lives between heaven and earth, benefiting from the way of heaven above and of earth below, while sharing in the two qi of yin and yang. Thus, human beings themselves also have a capacity for synergy, a capacity to initiate change. It is for this reason that humankind can be placed alongside heaven and earth—what is called "being a triad with heaven and earth"(yutiandican 与天地参)—to form the threefold structure of heaven, earth, and humankind.[5] Yet in the end, humankind is but the emulator of heaven and earth, and can only implement the way of nature. We cannot become natural legislators like the autonomous self as imagined by Kant. Therefore, the correct term for the human being is "person" (ren 人) rather than "subject" (zhuti 主体). That humankind is at the pinnacle of all that exists is not because we bravely overstep our authority to transcend other things, or that we are somehow able to establish a law for other things according to our own measure. It is because we can discard the self and follow things. It is because we can go beyond the bounds of our own selves and take all things as our measure, and in this way, share in the way of heaven and earth.

The Chinese spiritual world probably began in the Neolithic era and was firmly in place by the Zhou dynasty. The *Book of Changes* is an ancient history book and is also a methodology for existence. As Confucius says, "As for the *Book of Changes*, it inaugurates things and accomplishes doings, and encapsulates the way of tianxia, and nothing more."[6] The way of heaven is the way of the myriad things generating and regenerating without end. It is the way of being through change. "The way of tianxia" means the transformation of the way of heaven into the human way, and thus humankind generates and regenerates without end, and our virtue is a match with that of heaven and earth. The *Book of Changes* that explains the way of *tianxia* has become China's methodology of existence. It has so deeply entered the hearts of people that they may not even be aware of it in their daily life. It is the method of being through becoming, a way of seizing the opportunity between persistence and change. It is to anticipate what will happen and to act while it is still not raining: "to act from what has not yet happened, and to put in order before there is disorder."[7] It is to first actively change yourself before the extreme of change is reached in order to meet change with change. In so doing, you follow the flow of circumstances and lessen its impact. To make "change" into "bringing about change," you take the changes that happen to you and transform their "exteriority" into a force for change that you can use. This kind of taking the pattern of change and persistence and transforming it into a way of guiding change is observable in virtually all walks of life: in running a state, in deploying troops, in methods of production, in managing a household, in intercourse with other people, in dealing with things, in music, poetry, calligraphy, and even in chess and the martial arts. All forms of conduct follow the isomorphic method of "change and bringing about change." The *Book of Changes* calls it, "persistence through change" (*biantong* 变 通). Confucianism calls it, "the ability to adapt to change" by choosing the middle path.[8] Daoism says it is being like water since "there is nothing that can be used in its stead."[9] Each school has its own way of putting it, but they are all saying the same thing. The key to the way of transformation is "bringing about change." If it was merely a matter of being subject to change, it would simply be adapting to an external environment. But it is in fact the historical creative process of bringing about change that enables us to share in the workings of heaven and earth.[10] China uses the method of change and bringing about change to exist and to create a spiritual world. This would suggest that the basic principles of China's spiritual world are its method rather than a doctrine. As everyone knows, each dynasty in history had its own law code and each place its own customs. Over the course of history, customs and habits have changed. Change, both in the past and today, leads to renewal. It would be a great pity if we were then unable to accept any teaching or text from the past because today we have laid aside the ways that the Western Zhou used to attract distant peoples, or because we no longer can appreciate how the pre-Qin people were ready to give up life and forget death, or because we have difficulty understanding how the Tang and Song pressed on to their successes. Only by keeping to the old methodology of always seeking change can we hope for constant renewal and to allow life to flourish anew.

To interpret China's spiritual world as a methodology requires that we discover its original starting point, the point from which its path of thought begins. The precondition for all possible life is set by the combination of heaven and earth, wherein the role of heaven and earth is not open to question. It is only the actions of human beings who are situated between heaven and earth that produce the questions that require reflection. This means that heaven and earth are an unproblematic standard while it is human beings who create difficulties. What human beings do are called "doings," and among these doings, productive growth within *tianxia* is called "the grand undertaking" and is the most important of all doings.[11] Since "doings" are the very starting point that leads to all questions requiring thought, we can say, "I do therefore I am." Descartes took "I think therefore I am" (*cogito ergo sum*) as the first axiom of philosophy. In fact, if nothing was done then there could be no thought. Therefore, the first axiom of philosophy should be "I act therefore I exist" (*facio ergo sum*), since this alone conforms to the reality of existence.[12] All doings take existence as their first question. What existence seeks is nothing else than to continue to exist, to exist in perpetuity. This is the question of ceaseless generation and regeneration. The process of generation and regeneration cannot continue on its own but requires of the myriad things that they synergistically generate and regenerate. This is the way of nature. When it comes to human doings, generation and regeneration must occur together with other people. Hence generation and regeneration must transcend the question of simple existence and develop into the question of how to live a life. Life itself obeys a necessary principle, while a way of living opens up the possibilities for doing. Therefore, the shift from the question of life itself to that of a way of living means a shift from a principle of necessity to that of the possibilities of doing. The emergence of possibility is the very point at which existence breaks out and goes beyond its boundaries. As soon as existence transcends necessity and enters into possibility, it has a future. And when it has a future then there are doings to be done. In other words, once there is a future, "to be" becomes "to do."

By furthering the comparison with how Western philosophy goes about pursuing its basic problems, we may be able to follow the thread of this notion of "doings" more clearly. The starting point of Western philosophy is "things," that is, complete and fully formed beings. All things follow the same principle and form an ordered world, the cosmos. Therefore, the root question for thinking to engage is the origin of all that exists. Reflection on the origin is not directed at the origin of the world or at all things as such but seeks the cause of existence itself. For the most part, there are two questions: Why does something exist? and What is it that makes the being what it is? Herein lies an implied linguistic factor in Western thought. In Western languages, existence and being are two sides of the same question. A thing exists and is one thing rather than another. To exist is to be something. Where there is the existence of a thing then there is its substance, that is, the immutability that affirms the thing is indeed itself. Substance must be eternally immutable; otherwise it would not be this thing, but some other thing. Therefore, substance determines the exclusive and closed nature of the thing. In other words, it results in a clear definition of the thing in logical terms. If a concept suffices to fully express the totality, the independence, and the necessity of a thing, then it is an ideal. And the expression of the ideal of a substance is what knowledge seeks and wherein truth lies. The pattern of knowledge or truth is "what is what." From this we can understand why the spirit of Western thinking occupies itself with questions such as existence, reality, eternity, substance, perfection, logic, necessity, and certainty. Given that the focus for Western thought is on "things," it must examine things to look for their principles. The knowledge of concrete things attained by examining the nature (*physis*) of each and every thing belongs to physics, the old name for science. The province of philosophy then is the rational study of the origin of things and an explanation of the unchanging principles by means of which all things exist wherein the root principle is logic.

Unlike Western thought, the starting point for Chinese thought is "doings." Doing is not a thing but a dynamic relationship among things. Doing comes from acting. Therefore, it seeks its way in action. There are norms by which the way can be followed: rites, teaching, laws, and measures. These roughly do the work done by the norms (*nomos*) of the West. The way by means of which all doings are in motion and change is the way that lies above form—that of metaphysics. The types of question raised by Chinese and Western metaphysics differ, but both are matters of profound thought. In terms of the direction that thought takes, Western philosophy is thinking that deals with necessity, while Chinese philosophy is thinking that deals with possibility. In terms of the structure of thought, Western philosophy provides a "dictionary" kind of explanation of the of the world, seeking to set up an accurate understanding of the limits of all things. In simple terms, it determines "what is what" and all concepts are footnotes to "being" or "is." Chinese thought, however, is an explanation of the "grammar" of the world, striving for a coordinated understanding of the relationships—between heaven and humankind, humankind and things, or humans and humans—by which all doings are generated, with a special emphasis on the mutuality of relationships, and the compatibility of all things. Hence, the terms "persistence through change," "harmony," and "the mean and harmony" mentioned by the ancients are all insight-fully gathered under the notion of "proper measure" (*du* 度) by Li Zehou. Even so, the ancient thinkers of China were not without some discussion of "what is what." Confucius's theory of names and realities insists on the importance of delimitation. Yet, clearly "what becomes what" is the root question, since all questions are a response to "becoming." In other words, the "becoming" produces doing, and doing produces questions. On the other hand, absence of change implies nothing is done, and if nothing is done, then there are no questions. Therefore, within the framework of Chinese philosophy, the immutable substance of existence—assuming that things do indeed have a substance—does not give rise to any question, since it is just a judgment on their recurring sameness. In this sense, whatever gives rise to questioning is an opening up of possibilities: change, generation, the future, uncertainty, interaction, compatibility, and complementarity, and so on.

Going further, we can say that change is what the way of heaven naturally is. Since the way of heaven is a presupposition and not a ques-tion, change itself is not a question but the state accorded to what exists. It is only in responding to change that questions are formed, that is, it is only when people do things in response to change that questions are created. In other words, given that the way runs so of itself, whenever an existent is able to take itself as its own norm is not a question, and thus the way of heaven is not a question. At least it is not a question for humankind, though it may be a question for the creator. Instead, the way of heaven is a nonnegotiable norm. What human beings think and reflect on is how to shape the human way and match that of heaven within the limiting conditions set by the way of heaven. The primary question for the human way is that of generation and regeneration, and the first step herein is growth. This is the starting point for the evolutionary thread of Chinese thought. The "doing" of growth must seek what a thing relies on to be "deeply rooted and firmly planted"[13] in its growth. Therefore, growth first of all requires putting down roots. The two metaphors of growth and putting down roots set out the path for Chinese thought.

The appeal to growth and putting down roots are most probably related to early China's agricultural life. In agriculture, growth is what matters most. In the eyes of people who rely for a living on the growth of crops, existence lies in growth, or again, growth is existence. The doings of growth open up the question of existential time. In primitive ways of life when it was not necessary to worry about the growth of crops, time was a limitless quantity that need not be measured. What matters, though, with the question of the time of growth is not the abstract quantity of the arrow of time flying at an even speed, but the rhythm of fast and slow periods, changes in shape and form, opportunities that are lost and cannot be recovered, and gains and losses in an uncertain future. At the same time, the matter of growth leads to a new understanding of space. A growing plant must put its roots down in an unmoving place: crops put down roots; farmers fix their residences. And thus people cannot move in space but must wait in time, and in unchanging space they must respond to the myriad changes in time: "The one who makes the most of persistence in change is one who seizes the right time."[14] Life moves in accordance with the commands of time, according to the four seasons, the seasonal nodes,[15] the rising and setting of the sun, the waxing and waning of the moon. All of these opportunities give rise to moments in which to decide what to do. The way of life of walking in step with the rhythm of the changes of time and maintaining a point of relative stillness, and maintaining a definite relationship with that which is not definite, reveals a principle of change in which the myriad changes and what is not changing are united as one. Given that existence is growth itself, the question the kind of thinking that takes growth as its main theme must necessarily reflect upon is the way of growth's daily renewal. The way of growth is the way of existence, and taking it one step further, it extends to the way of human doings and then finally is realized as the way of morality, politics, history, and aesthetics. Therefore, despite the fact that since ancient times China's institutions were at some point in time set, there is no absolute determinative principle. The only unchanging rule is the art of persistence through change. In this sense, the ultimate goal of Chinese thought is not the truth of logic, but the art of growth.

The art of growth is an ontology, and not one of the fine arts. Yet, this ontology of existence at the same time reveals itself as an aesthetic demonstration, prompting Confucius to say that life is "consummated by music."[16] This would seem to imply that the metaphysics of growth can also be manifested in the world of phenomena. As such, growth is a form of rejoicing, becoming the source of rejoicing about the interrelated growth of the myriad things. This explains why there are among the six classics the *Odes* and *Music* that are directly related to aesthetics. "Music" is not restricted to music as such but is used in the general sense of all aesthetic experience. There is a permeating musicality that moves in step with the rhythmical changes of the way of heaven that is the music of growth. Han Linde has an insight with respect to this: China has an aestheticizing understanding of all things and all doings. This aesthetic understanding is temporal and musical in nature and may be termed a "musical cosmology" or "the musicalization of the cosmos."[17] This is what the ancients meant in saying, "Music is the harmony of heaven and earth" and "great music has the same harmony as heaven and earth."[18] Therefore, the movement of images in poetry is a kind of musicality, and so too are the brush strokes in calligraphy, and likewise the wandering footpaths through the mountains and valleys, and the cycles of rising and falling in history, and the repetition of the seasons of heaven and earth. Indeed, all experience seeks after a musical rhythm in its growth.

Agriculture binds life to the soil and makes the natural earth become the site of growth, "the native land" (*xiangtu* 乡土), and in reverse, the native land then becomes the spiritual ground of existence. Fei Xiaotong (1910–2005) defines the Chinese spirit as being "from the soil," what might be called an authoring of vitality.[19] Human reliance on the soil accords a spirituality to the land. The land is no longer a place for slow wanderings to distant places but the great earth mother. "*Kun* is the earth, and is thus called the 'mother.' "[20] "The substantiality of *kun* enables it to carry things."[21] Therefore, in the picture of life, nature is certainly not some object of one amorphous body but is divided into two kinds of spirit: that of heaven and that of earth. Heaven is the universal sponsor of the existence of the myriad things while earth is the special sponsor of the existence of each person. Since the soil is the homeland of existence, keeping watch over the land amounts to keeping watch over the root. Thus, this land—that is, the land that is the root—becomes a spiritual concept, and keeping watch over the land also becomes a sacred responsibility. This land is not only the soil in which the crops put down roots, it is also the home where persons put down their roots. Even though the home that one has set up is only a small part of the world, still it has one share of a complete life. It follows, then, that to own a home is to own a complete world, and people who own a world do not need to travel far.[22] Those persons who take the earth as their mainstay look up and read the celestial signs, look down and observe the topography of the land, and survey all four directions of *tianxia*. This kind of looking up, down, and in all directions, produces an image of a world that is fixed in one place and expands outward without limit. Or we could also say, it is a visual and sensory image of the entire world that can then be transformed into standing at the center of the earth and taking in a political vision of the whole *tianxia*—an idea closely related to China as the Middle Country. As the *Book of Changes* says:

> Of old when Bao Xi ruled over *tianxia*, looking up, he observed the symbols in the heavens, looking down, he observed the norms of the earth, he observed the patterns of birds and beasts and the properties of the earth. Near at hand, he became aware of his own person, and far away he became aware of all things. And from this he began to create the eight trigrams in order to penetrate the power of all mysteries and to categorize the qualities of the myriad things.[23]

The worldview that surveys everything under the sun—the eight waste-lands and the six directions—is the conception of *tianxia*.[24] This kind of worldview, gazing up and down and all around the four quarters, in the same way transforms to become a way of taking the aesthetic measure of the myriad things. Han Linde analyzes this as follows: "The Chinese [*huaxia*] people's view of heaven and earth and the myriad things is one of searching upward and scrutinizing downward, the movement of a gaze that brings a penetrating of the horizon and inspecting what is near into one body, and a line of sight that has a fluid compass constantly moving back and forth and from near to far."[25] Fan Xiwen of the Southern Song was perhaps the earliest person to reflect on how this kind of aesthetic gaze of taking everything in was universally present in poetry and painting.[26]

We understand things in order to understand "doings." Natural change is only its temporality, while the changes of human doings cut out a human measurement for time that is historical in nature. Hence it is said, "Things have roots and branches; doings have beginnings and endings."[27] "Things" belong to the category of necessity, and being fundamentally lacking in history, have only roots and branches. "Doings" belong to the category of possibility, and having beginnings and endings, shape history. Thus, with the world of things, there is only epistemology, whereas it is only with the world of doings that it produces the question of an ontology that is related to human beings. In logical terms, the world of things also has the question of ontology, but that is a question that belongs to the creator, and not one that humankind can usurp and talk nonsense about. It is only in the world of doings that human beings can be masters. Thus, the question of ontology produced by doings is at the same time a question of human creativity, that is, the creating of the possibilities in life, and of creating history.[28] Doings are not governed by necessity; what doings open up are possibilities. That is, doings give existence a matrix of possibilities, and where there are possibilities, there is a future and a history. Each moment of the future contains many possible options. Therefore, different doings create different futures. Jorge Luis Borges in "The Garden of Forking Paths" calls it "the forking of time." He imagines a Chinese architect of ancient times who constructed a labyrinth of forking paths within a garden. The garden of forking paths is a metaphor for the forking paths of time. The Chinese architect "did not believe in a uniform, absolute time. He believed in an infinite series of times, in a growing, dizzying network of divergent, convergent, and parallel times."[29] It is for this reason that "time is forking perpetually toward innumerable futures."[30] Borges's understanding of the key points of Chinese thought is really quite accurate. The question of each thing turns on the future possibilities defined by the forked paths of time and opens up from there. The future of the forked paths of time always appears as one unique doing at one unique moment, but as soon as, in the flow of doings, one single word of the narrative splits into many histories, it returns to the forking of time. This moment is a reality that is gone in a flash, a liminal point, and what lies before us are the forked paths of the future, while what lies behind are the forked paths of history.

Given that one half of a doing is the future and the other half is history, there are two decisive matters of great significance for human beings who live in the world: "creative making" (zuo 作) and "narrating" (shu 述). These two things give meaning to all things and ensure that the future and history are self-conscious. Chinese characters are imagistic hieroglyphs, and thus ancient characters always retain in some degree the original form of the "doing"—though there are many characters that have already become difficult to decipher. The original form of the doing must be something that really has an impact for it to become a model containing an important message for life. In the oracle bone script, the character 作 (zuo "creating, doing") is written as ▉ and was originally the character zha 乍 that is written as �. There is as yet no general consensus as to what the original character zuo depicts.[31] From the divinations performed, its main meanings are verbal: "making," "establishing," "creating," and the like, that are similar to its later meaning of "creating." From this we can imagine that whatever was chosen as the original model for the character zuo must have been the creation of an important thing used in everyday life. Xu Zhongshu suggests that the diagram is one that depicts "the first making of the collar of a robe."[32] This is one possibility. However, just by looking at the old form of the character, we may also imagine that it depicts the action of a farm implement. For instance, one version looks like a shovel just about to be put into the untouched soil—the foot would be forcefully pressed on the horizontal part to push it in. Or it could be the action of removing weeds, or even that of a plow breaking open the earth, or something similar. One form of the character has what looks like the forked branch of a plant and may indicate the crops that are about to sprout up, or it could be that weeds are being dug up. All these images have to do with labor in the fields. Clothing and food are the root of life and both are highly important creations, and so both could be options. Although it is not easy to choose, yet if we must, then I tend toward the image of agricultural labor. The reason for this is that the business of agriculture must surely hold a prominent place in daily life. The creative activity of agriculture leads crops to grow, and this would have been the most immediate model of creating that would come to mind for early man. Moreover, the key activities of zuo are more closely related to growth than to anything else: that is, the creating of the future. In any case, whatever is depicted by the graph zuo, and this would require the confirmation of experts, the meaning seems to be consistent. All alike take zuo to mean the creating of the doings that constitute a life.

In metaphysical terms, what zuo creates is the future. It takes the many possibilities of the future and limits them to produce one reality. Likewise, what shu (narrating) writes down is history. It opens up the one past action into a complex history, changing this reality into many kinds of strands and threads that can then forever be cited. Thus, it is human beings who are the creators of the future—and of history. Of course, not all doings in life can be called creative actions. The scope defined by "doings" is for the most part limited to the kind of behavior that is deliberate and planned. The scope of creative activity is limited to creative doings, or more strictly speaking, creativity that is going to transform time into history. That is, it is only actions that formulate and enact laws with respect to modes of existence and ways of living and that leave traceable marks on time that can be considered "creative actions." What is significant here is that creative doing means what originally only had a temporal existence takes on both a future and a history. The creative doing that establishes the laws for existence is the conduct of creating history, or said another way, it is a conduct whereby human beings create a world. Thus, creative doing has ontological significance. The creation of history is generally ascribed to the deeds of sages illustrated by the classical examples that follow here.

The *Book of Changes* has a passage that narrates the great creative doings of ancient times:

> Of old when Bao Xi ruled over *tianxia*, looking up, he observed the symbols in the heavens, looking down, he observed the norms of the earth, he observed the patterns of birds and beasts and the properties of the earth. Near at hand, he became aware of his own person, and far away he became aware of all things. And from this he began to create the eight trigrams in order to penetrate the power of all mysteries and to categorize the qualities of the myriad things. He knotted strings into coarse nets and fine nets, for hunting and fishing. . . . After Bao Xi died, the Divine Farmer acted. He cut trees to make plowshares and bent wood to make handles. The benefits of plowing and hoeing were taught to *tianxia*. . . . At midday he set up markets, bringing the people of *tianxia* together, gathering the goods of *tianxia* in one place. Once exchanges had been made they retired and each went to his place. . . . When the Divine Farmer had passed, the Yellow Emperor, Yao, and Shun continued his innovations. They fathomed the persistence through change of the world around them and saved the people from exhaustion. Through spiritual insight (*shen*) they transformed the human experience and enabled the

people to find what was most fitting in their lives. According to the *Changes*, with everything running its course, there is flux (*bian*), where there is such flux, there is continuity (*tong*), and where there is such continuity, it is enduring. By this means they were helped by heaven. Good fortune came and there was nothing that was not beneficial. The Yellow Emperor, Yao, and Shun wearing shirt and robe brought order to *tianxia*. . . . They hollowed out trees and made them into boats, cut wood for oars. The benefit of boats and oars was to row to places where they could not before, and reaching distant shores they could benefit *tianxia*. . . . They trained oxen and yoked horses in order that heavy things could be carried to distant places and benefit *tianxia*. . . . They made double doors and introduced the warning of the wooden clapper to anticipate marauding visitors. . . . They cut wood for pestles and dug the earth to make mortars. The benefits of pestle and mortar provided help to the myriad peoples. . . . They tensed wood with string to make a bow and cut wood for arrows. The benefits of bow and arrow occasioned awe in all *tianxia*. . . . In ancient times people dwelt in caves or in the open wasteland, but in later generations the sages changed these dwellings into palaces and rooms. Above there was the roof beam and below the eves projected outward to ward off wind and rain. . . . In ancient times the dead were covered with branches and laid out in the open wastelands. There was no mound raised and no trees planted and no fixed time for the period of mourning. In later generations, the sages changed this for the inner and outer coffins. . . . In ancient times, memory strings were knotted to carry on government. In later generations, the sages changed these for writing on wooden tablets by which the hundred officials governed and the business of the myriad peoples was examined.[33]

Again, the *Book of History* records:

Yao was able to make the noble and virtuous shine out such that love went to the nine ranks of kin. The nine ranks of kin were harmonious. He pacified the people of a hundred surnames. The people of a hundred surnames shone with intelligence. He harmonized and gathered in one the myriad states. The black-haired people were transformed. He then commanded Xi and He, who reverently honored the august heaven, to record in a calendar the appearances of sun, moon, stars, and asterism, respectfully establishing seasons for the people.[34]

While the *Hanfeizi* writes about creative actions:

In ancient times, people were few and birds and beasts many. People could not overcome birds, beasts, insects, or snakes. A sage offered his creations. He shaped wood into nests to provide shelter from what would do them harm and the people rejoiced in this, so that he reigned over *tianxia* and his sobriquet was "Nest Builder." The people ate fruit, gourds, mussels, and clams. These reeked with a bad smell and injured their intestines, and many of the people fell ill and were sick. A sage offered his creations. He drilled with a stick and made fire and thus got rid of the bad smell and the people rejoiced in this, so that he reigned over *tianxia* and his sobriquet was "Fire Stick Man."[35]

The *Guanzi* also talks about creative actions:

Fuxi created and made the six trigrams of heaven and earth to correspond to *yin* and *yang*. He created the number 9 x 9 to match the way of heaven and *tianxia* changed accordingly. The Divine Farmer created and planted the five grains on the sunny slopes of Mount Qi; the people of the nine regions then became acquainted with cereal food and *tianxia* changed accordingly. The Yellow Emperor created, using a fire stick in a hole to make fire so as to cook smelly meat; when the people ate it, they did not get stomach pains, and *tianxia* changed accordingly.[36]

Mr. *Lü's Spring and Autumn Annals* also talks about creation:

Xi Zhong created carts. Cang Jie created writing. Hou Ji created cereals. Gao Yao created punishments. Kun Wu created pots.

Xia Gun created walled towns. These six persons all created what was proper. Yet these were none of them masters of the way and so it is said they were creators.[37]

Also, the *Huainanzi*: "Of old, Cang Jie created writing and heaven rained on the crops, and the spirits wailed in the night."[38]

There are many similar passages on creation in the ancient books. Of special interest is that the *Shiben* dedicates a separate section to creation that in particular records all the epoch-making technological creations of the ancients found in the legends, including that of the Fire Stick Man creating fire, Fu Xi creating the tabular cithara, Wang creating the net, the Divine Farmer mixing drugs to save people, Chi You creating weapons, the Yellow Emperor creating the fringed cap, Ling Lun making pitch pipes, Rong Cheng making the calendar, Cang Jie creating writing, Shi Huang creating maps, Yu Ze creating sandals, Yong Fu creating the pestle and mortar and taming oxen, Xiang Tu creating the yoking of horses, Gong Gu and Huo Di creating boats, Wu Peng creating medicine, Zhu Rong creating markets, Xi Zhong creating carts, and the like.[39] Among these innovations, most of the basic forms of technology necessary for early civilization are attributed to the Yellow Emperor himself or to his ministers. According to Qi Sihe, five creations are attributed to the Yellow Emperor in the *zuo pian* of the *Shiben* while twenty-three are ascribed to his ministers, making a total of twenty-eight in all. Although these reports are not necessarily historical facts, yet virtually all of them can be supported by secondary evidence from other books.[40] This would seem to imply that the period of the Yellow Emperor was an era rich in creativity.

The ancients in their understanding of *zuo* or "creative doing" set their standard as kind of institutional creativity in introducing some great innovation, and they frequently appealed to the examples of the establishing of directives by the sage kings. The creation of technology was seen as an important and indeed necessary type of creation, but it did not rise to the standard of creating institutions, or said another way, "it was not kingly governance." For this reason, there was only the creator, a person who discovered something at a special moment in time. But, this politicization of the standard raises some doubts. The creation of institutions is certainly of enormous value, but from the long view of history, the creation of technology, whether of boats and carts, of houses and moats and city walls, has a profound and long-lasting influence on civilization. They are not something that can be assessed in terms of the effects of a single moment, and with them there are some creative triumphs that go beyond politics. And especially with agriculture and the invention of writing, such innovations cannot be reduced to mere technology. Rather they are great accomplishments that open up the way and establish new norms, and they have an importance that is difficult to match. In fact, creativity in all aspects of civilization makes its contribution to opening up the way and establishing new norms, and are all innovations in the way humankind can exist. Hence, all of these are epoch-changing, major events in history.

Shu (narrating) is the spelling out of *zuo* (creative doing). What history stores up is far, far less than the facts of what really happened. Not everything needs to be recorded, and because people lack the capacity to record everything that transpires, only the major events and happenings are remembered by history. Making a record and narrating also have their differences. All important events that have an ongoing influence on life are worth recording, but not all things that must be recorded are worth narrating. The facts that are recorded become the notebooks of history while those that are narrated form the way of history. In other words, the facts that must be narrated have to do with the creation of ways of existence, and the order of existence. In this sense, history constitutes the traces of creating. The creative inventions of the ancients do not become beneficial to the life of later generations only in a material sense, they also work on the spiritual level to become a way of thinking for contemporary people. Hence, through narration, the creations of the ancients transcend the flow of time, and begin and end on the stage. This beginning and ending refers to a spirit, and it becomes the spiritual basis by means of which later generations continue to exist and create. Therefore, the creations of the ancients are the being of later generations. Being as such and such is not as it is by virtue of the immutable substance of the thing itself, but because "creative doing" makes something what it is. In terms of the doings of humankind, it is through creating that being is able to become existence, and through narrating, creating is able to continue to exist. The continuity of spirit lies in creativity being transformed into narration. As Zhang Xuecheng (1738–1801) has put it, creating is the establishing of norms; narrating is the establishing of a doctrine. Each makes its own contribution, with "the one who creates being a sage, and the one who establishes a doctrine being a teacher."[41] There is no greater legislator than the Duke of Zhou and no greater teacher than Confucius. Therefore, "Before the Sui and Tang dynasties, the academy offered sacrifices equally to the Duke of Zhou and to Confucius, seeing the Duke as the foremost sage and Confucius as the foremost teacher."[42] After the rise of the School of Principle in the Song and Ming eras, the tradition was narrated anew, saying more about Confucius and Mencius. People put more stress on narrating as opposed to creating. There was an objective reason for this. After the Qin and Han dynasties, there were no earth-shattering political revolutions that affected the way, but only changes in policy. Hence, significant creations were seldom seen, referencing here only legislative issues, since in the fields of engineering, art, poetry, literature, calligraphy, and architecture there were many significant creations. Zhang Xuecheng believed that in fact, ever since the Duke of Zhou created the classical administrative order, there was very little else that could be created. Despite all of his ability and virtue, even Confucius held no post and had no authority to create a new order. Instead he wholeheartedly "followed the Zhou" and did not create. He simply "narrated rather than created" and through narration established his teachings.[43]

However, there is another possible explanation for this turn from creation to narration. Sima Qian suggests that the achievements of Confucius cannot all be ascribed to narrating because Confucius's narration was in fact a kind of spiritual legislation that was indeed creation: "He discussed the *Book of Odes* and the *Book of History* and compiled the *Spring and Autumn Annals*. Scholars take these as their norms even today."[44] Even though Confucius in establishing his teachings did not set up any administrative norms, he did give us spiritual norms. Sima Qian's view, however, would seem to be more than this, although he does not explain his reasons in any great detail. I would like to speculate on his reasons as follows. In compiling (*zuo* creating) the *Spring and Autumn Annals*, Confucius affirmed the supreme and irreplaceable status of historical consciousness and historical learning in the Chinese spiritual world, virtually making history itself into a belief. For this reason, China takes history as its spiritual basis and uses history to interpret the purpose and meaning of life. The historical books have become China's "Holy Bible."[45] Thus it is said, "The Six Classics are all history."[46] Of course, Confucius was not the originator of historical consciousness, but the one who established its norms. China's own narration of its spiritual world was originally a historical narration. The *Book of Changes*, the *Book of History*, and the *Book of Odes* are all ancient historical books. Confucius in compiling the

Spring and Autumn Annals established a universal norm for the narration of history, namely, that the way of human beings must conform to the way of heaven. The deep meaning invested in the way in which the *Spring and Autumn Annals* was written lies in how the most insignificant expression reveals that, in any possible way of living, we must tacitly acknowledge the way of heaven. It thus guarantees that life becomes a possible manner of living within the order of being. The real meaning of the *Spring and Autumn Annals* is that the way of heaven is held up as a mirror that reveals what order can be changed and what order cannot.[47] Clearly, there is no order that cannot be changed; otherwise there would be no way to explain the legitimacy of the revolutions of Tang against the Xia, and Wu against the Shang. But such a change in order must conform to the way of heaven.[48] Confucius turns the metaphysical principle of conformity to heaven into a principle of history. Thus, history and thought became as one: "The ancients never gave reasons that did not conform to what they did."[49] Furthermore, historicity became the core question to ponder, and the six classics became China's "Holy Bible."

Though history narrates things of the past, yet its meaning is for the future. If there were no future then the issue of the meaning of history would not arise, and the past would be confined to the chronicles of what was over and done with. History that is no longer productive becomes ancient relics that are at one remove from life. Such history has nothing to say to life, just as crops that cannot grow contribute nothing. What is the termination of history? It is to deny the possibility of a future. To say farewell to possibility is to say farewell to a meaningful world, for meaning is determined by possibility, while necessity determines truth. The problem is that a world that only has truths is a meaningless world. The existence of something meaningless is itself held in a relationship of cause and effect, and thus is subject to change. But this kind of necessary change through cause and effect denies possibility. Even if there is a yet-to-come, there is no future. There would only be unlimited time. The significance implied by possibility lies only in the future that is produced in the changing discourse of past and present. That is, only in the possibility related to the meaning generated by past and present is a future generated. We might also say that only in the possibility of constructing a destiny can there be a future.

Awareness of time lies in the awareness of the contrast between the past and the future, shaped by the ever-flowing focal point of this moment. This differs from the subjective division of time into three parts: past, present, and future. The twofold division—past and present—expresses the historical sense of time. It separates history into two, but not time. The future has not yet come onto the stage; it still remains outside past and present. Although the future lies outside past and present, yet in it lies the full significance of past and present. Were there no future, the present would mark an end, and the past would, as a result, lose its meaning. The life or death of meaning depends on the ability to grow and continue. For instance, an ancient script that is completely unreadable is meaningless, nothing more than a dead relic of the past that can no longer produce anything whatsoever. China also has other ways of expressing temporality: "in ancient times" (xi 昔) and "about to come" (lai 来). However, these terms do not express a subjective awareness of time, or the idea of natural time. They are rather the memory of past natural changes and the portent of future change. Even though they are not history, they still depict a kind of "natural history" and thus come close to history. Perhaps they presage the historical consciousness of past and present. Tracing this to its source, the form of the character 昔 (xi "in ancient times") appears on the oracle bone inscriptions as 昔: the upper part depicts waves of water while the lower part depicts the sun. Sometimes the order is inverted but the meaning is the same. The general supposition is that the depiction for xi is based on the memory of a great flood.[50] We can imagine that for the early people of the Central Plain, the memory of a great flood would have left a deep impression, and the idea could easily have been used to refer to the past. Furthermore, a metaphysical interpretation of the form of the character could see it as expressing Confucius's sigh: "Isn't life's passing just like this, never ceasing day or night!"[51] Likewise, it could be used to refer to the past. The character 来 (lai "about to come") on the oracle bone script is written as 来, and all scholars agree it is the image of a cereal plant. Most take it to be wheat.[52] That it is a plant is certainly true, though its identification as wheat is not confirmed, only highly probable. There was already wheat in the Shang dynasty, but it was not yet the most important crop, or the most ancient. But these are irrelevant considerations. The important thing is that crops imply the process of work and harvesting. The growth of crops implies the expectation of a harvest. Whether one can expect a harvest depends on the workings of heaven. Therefore, farm labor gives a new identity to the future: the future is a possibility that can be anticipated. Therefore, the meaning of the future spills over into the idea of natural time, and a possible future is differentiated from the necessary yet-to-come of a scheduled succession of present moments. The rising and setting of tomorrow's sun is not a question that needs discussion with human beings: whether or not they wait for it, it will certainly come.[53] Wheat is a portent of things to come. If one has not offended against heaven, insects, or the dragon king, it will become a reality. Therefore, the concept of the future defined by wheat carries the question of destiny, and destiny points to history.

The past is an epistemological question; the future is a metaphysical question. The future does not yet exist and hence cannot be the object of knowledge. But the future is a question that requires planning and hence is a metaphysical question. Mozi made a very meaningful remark: "If you have planned to no avail, then you must use what is past to know the future, and must use what is seen to know what is hidden."[54] The future holds many uncertain possibilities and is not something that can be fixed through human planning. Planning lies with human beings; the outcome lies with heaven. Yet since people must plan the future, they can only rely on the experience of the past. They take realities that can be seen to understand possibilities that cannot be seen. This suggests that, taken as a metaphysical question, the future cannot have a certain response. But it can have a historical resolution, that is, the metaphysical question can be transformed into a historical question. Using experience to wait for the future is like waiting for the ripening of wheat. Farmwork should lead to a harvest, but one still has to have suitable winds and rain. Even in ancient times, when experience was as stable and reliable as gold, knowing the future from the past was still not perfectly reliable, and so at bottom we must say that the future must be an object that is constantly up for discussion. Experience is the thread by which a discussion with the future is carried on, but when circumstances change and experience fails, there must be creative actions to deal with the way of existence, and the path of the future must be redefined. At the same time, this is to create history. Therefore, we can say that ontology is also "creationology." Mozi's "you must use what is past to know the future" is only half of the question of the future; the other half is "to open up what is to come by doing."

The question of "doing" transcends the natural structure of "in ancient times—about to come" and opens up the historical dimension of "past and present." The arrival of the future not only needs presuppositions built on experience but also requires the opening up provided by creating. "Doing" transforms inactive being into proactive becoming.

"Doing" is both a break in the state of existence and a continuation of existence. It changes undifferentiated *chronos* into differentiated *kairos*. Here time gains a rhythm and becomes history. Since "coming" and "doing" constitute the core question of ontology, only when the time to come is no longer a repetition of the past, but is the continuation of existence with doing as a variable, does existence have a history. The ontology defined by the relationship of coming and doing is the point of intersection between epistemology and metaphysics, and is the turning point where the question of time becomes the question of history. "Doing" creates the variable for the ontological turning point. That is to say, "doing" enables time to get the historical calibration between past and present. Any future can be transformed into past and present because of "doing." Natural life originally only had the temporal measurement of "in ancient times" and "about to come," but "doing" defines the historical measurement of past and present. On the natural structure of "in ancient times" and "about to come" is built the historical structure of past and present and thus creates the two kinds of temporal consciousness: natural time and historical time.

The deep meaning of the idea of past and present is already implicit in the ancient Chinese character *gu* 古. The earliest form of this character in the oracle bone script was 𠮢, and later it was written as 𠱮. In the latter form, the upper stroke is a cross that was to become the character for the number ten. It means to be set up in the center, seeming to imply a determination of time in the exact center. According to Feng Shi, its original sense is a gnomon that casts a shadow, an image of the center and the four directions.[55] The lower part of the character *gu* depicts a mouth. The mouth can only give utterance to what is past. Combined with the cross, this means that the mouth speaks of what happened in the past in the four directions. This is what the past is.[56] In the oracle bone script, the character 今 (*jin* "present") is written as ⌂, a symbol of a wooden clapper, referencing an ancient form of bronze bell with a wooden tongue that kings and ministers used to announce they were about to issue orders.[57] The moment of announcing a decree in the "present" means that from this moment onward such an order must be carried out. From this we can see that *jin* not only means this moment but is also the *kairos* that is opened up by "doing." Hence, rather than saying that "present" is a measure of time, it would be better to call it a measure of history. The creative doing called "present" must by definition refer to a thing that is done, a beginning within life, or the beginning of some institution. Thus, the present has a historical temporality that includes the future. It is the "contemporariness" of historical temporality and not the "presentness" of temporal temporality.

The past and the present are both defined by the historical temporality of doing, referring respectively to the historical creativity of the past perfect tense and the historical creativity of the present perfect continuous tense. Thus, they are at odds with the natural temporality of "in ancient times" and "about to come." If something has not yet brought about a change, either in terms of society or institutions, then there is no new doing. In terms of history, this belongs to the past, even if in terms of time, it is actually in the present. By defining historicity in terms of past and present, a period of natural time could be very long and yet historically short. Likewise, a very short period of natural time could be very long historically. If an institution or a spirit never changes, it only has the contemporaneity of the present. For example, in the West, the tradition of universalism created by St. Paul still remains a spiritual model that is very much active. Alain Badiou argues for this.[58] Correctly speaking, the concept of "the present" (jin) expresses the present tense more clearly and more accurately than contemporaneity because the present clearly includes the future that is one with it, while contemporaneity emphasizes uniformity with the progress of time and fails to capture the future sense implied by "the present."

Turning to the past and present of China, we find that Sima Qian's study of the past and present occurs at the turn from the Zhou to the Qin, not merely a change of dynasties but of institutions. Therefore, it is a turn in historical tense and not simply the passage of time. According to the self-understanding of the Han people, political institutions from the time of the Yellow Emperor, Yao, and Shun up to that of the First Emperor of the Qin had not changed at all. Those institutions were the feudal institutions of tianxia that belonged wholly to the past. Although this understanding of the Qin and Han people was not accurate, yet it was not far from the mark. The feudal institutions of tianxia were the creation of the Zhou, since prior to the Zhou there was merely a system of alliances between the myriad states.[59] The First Emperor of Qin changed the feudal institutions of the lords into a unified empire of commanderies and counties. This huge institutional shift was a creative doing of historic proportions that matches the creative doing of the Duke of Zhou. In contrast to the historical tense of the past, the Qin opened up a "present" historical tense. If we simply take institutional turns to talk about past and present, then, the era from the Qin to Sima Qian can be seen as belonging to the present. The two thousand years after Sima Qian can still be seen as belonging to the present of Qin-Han institutions. Despite there being many superficial changes throughout these two thousand years, yet the basic institutions did not change, and so the period as a whole still belongs to the present of the Qin and Han. The present of the Qin and Han finally ended in the late Qing and became the past, but the present of contemporary China—since the time of Kang Youwei and Liang Qichao—is a present that has not yet settled into a fixed form. Therefore, for the past hundred years the many questions vexing China are still as new as ever, very much active in the historical tense of the present of contemporary China. An even more complicated question is that the game of globalization has brought contemporary China deeply into a present shared in common by the whole world. As a result, at this moment, China exists in two historical present times and is involved in two historical creative doings. This is something never seen before and the future it will bring is something that cannot be known.

Faced with the vicissitudes of history and its many changes, China has never let go of its ancestral roots. Part of this may be due to luck, but also to the decree of heaven. The term "decree of heaven" (tian-ming) is an ancient one that is tinged with mythology. As was noted, and as is understood today, the decree of heaven is a method. China's way of existing through change is grounded in the threefold unity of its ontology, methodology, and historical outlook, and the one thread of the way, creative doing, and narrating. Its core concept is the consistency among of the three notions of "change" (bianhua), "persistence through change" (biantong), and "consistency through change" (tongbian). In this, ontology is the body and methodology is function. The historical outlook is the self-awareness and self-narration of ontology and methodology. The reason why the method of existence through change can become the guarantee of the decree of heaven is that this method is one of responding to all possible changes, a method that can accept all kinds of possibilities and so cannot be deconstructed. A way of existence that cannot be deconstructed is the decree of heaven.

The ontology implicit in the *Book of Changes* is an ontology of becoming. Its way of thinking is very different from the ontology of being. As a noun referencing "the being" has, in fact, only a grammatical function and no meaning in reality. In reality, being can only be a verb (to be) or a participle (being) because the state of being is becoming. The core question of becoming is how to realize the basic meaning of existence, that is, how to enable existence to endure, the question of generation and regeneration. In reality, generation and regeneration is a question that has to do with the future, and the future is formed by innumerable possibilities. Therefore, existence is an existence at the center of possible changes. For this reason, what ontology studies is how to effectively apply the methodology of existence. The ancients used the way (*dao* 道) to refer to this, the passing on of the mysterious. The way of making existence effective lies in persistence in change. The key to persistence in change lies in consistency in the manipulating of change, changing as things change, maintaining an unchanging relationship with change, and thus staying on the good side of change. This is the way of change that combines the mutable and the immutable. Therefore, persistence in change cannot just remain on the good side, it can also enable change in existence to have greater capacity, such that it can respond to many, many changes, and in so doing, existence itself does not change. Laozi's *Daodejing* uses water as a metaphor to express the immutable nature of the way. The most effective way of existing is to be like water that takes the shape of whatever it encounters, that advances wherever the opportunity arises, and that by virtue of its weakness, can overcome what is hard. The methodology of water has entered deeply into human hearts and may perhaps explain why China is good at changing and good at existing. The China that is a way of growth has an infinite capacity for change. It is as if China can exist as a world, with the capacity for a global inclusiveness, and a method of growth that enables it to become what it previously was not.

The historical outlook that corresponds to the ontology of becoming and the methodology of persistence through change is the outlook of consistency through change, or what Sima Qian referred to as the historical understanding of the change that continues through the past and present. Consistency is the existence that runs as one through past and present, and it is the way in which the contemporaneity of the past and the present exist and come together. Since this runs through past and present, the past is no longer a denial, a rejection, or a sublimation of the past.[60] Rather, the past is transformed into the present, and the present is thereby enriched. If there is only change and no transformation, then there is merely a break with no continuity. Likewise, if the experience of the past cannot be transformed into a resource for the present, then the novelty of the day is made over into a loss. The quicker one goes, the shorter history becomes, and the more that meaning is impoverished. Therefore, the thread of the past becoming the present is the present being the continuous creative doing of the past. And though the present is a new creative doing, it must still contain the meaning of the past. This is the real meaning of upholding what is new. While upholding what is new may be a revolution in institutions and technology, its deepest significance lies in its continuing destiny, that is, in respecting the ongoing nature of being. History that runs through past and present and upholds what is new is indeed the way that responds to the unceasing generation and regeneration of change. It is clear that the historical outlook of consistency though change is unrelated to the regressive outlook and to the modern progressive outlook. We should say that an understanding of the historical outlook of consistency through change is completely outside the framework of progress and regress.[61]

What we should note is that what is described as the phenomena of progress and regress are completely different from progress and regress as theories, so much so that they should never be treated as one and the same. As descriptions, progress and regress are clearly phenomena that are beyond doubt. For example, today's technology has progressed many hundreds of times beyond that of the past while the poetry of today is thousands of times worse than the poetry of the Tang and Song dynasties. However, theories of progress and regress are theories of predestination, where the way changes take place follows an objective rule, presuming that the future is predestined, either by supposing that history has an ultimate aim or end point, or by believing in some fixed cycle. This kind of unproven determination of the future is a denial of the futurity of the future, that in denying the limitless possibilities of the future, thereby negates the significance of the idea of the future. The contemporary theory of progress that has been around since the Enlightenment, if misused and applied to any field at all outside that of scientific technology—including institutions, art, or values—becomes an antihistorical outlook. If new culture is the cause that can deny old culture, then history has no way of accumulating knowledge or maintaining its meaning. Each present is only a useful tool with respect to the next moment and can hardly escape the denial of destiny contained in the next moment.[62] Once, in accelerating denial, the meaning of history is being dissipated, then history will, at an accelerating rate, retract into insignificance and soon disappear.

What is built based on the historical outlook of the ontology of becoming is a historicity that is unlimited in its openness and, at the same time, able to run through change with an unlimited capacity to accumulate. Although its historical tense has the two ideas of past and present, yet the key lies in the present. The present is an active state that, on the one hand, accepts the wisdom of the past and changes the meaning of past creative doings into the present and, on the other hand, is a contemporaneity that is an active opening up and preserving, a smelting of the past to shape the present. The concept of the present defines something that differs from a natural consciousness of the flow of historical time. The natural consciousness of the flow of time may proceed from what was, to the future via the now. Or it may proceed from the future to what was, via the now. The present, however, means that historical time proceeds from what was to now, and from the future to now. That is, time travels toward the present from two directions, and as such the present becomes the focal point of time. If we say that the geographical center from which we look round in four directions is an image of the constructive potential of China, then the two-way openness of the present is a temporal center that constructs the awareness of continuity through change in China's enduring existence. The awareness of this continuity through change lies in that the present puts down deep roots and has the strength to grow and develop. The Chinese history that continues through change is one in which China's historical outlook of consistency through change attains to a self-consciousness of its own identity, and the tale of China continues.

The ancient Greek story of the ship of Theseus tells of a wooden ship where some of the boards are broken and had to be replaced by new ones. This process continues until all of the boards of the wooden ship are new and none of the old ones remain. And yet this wooden ship still looks exactly the same as the original wooden ship . . .

Notes

Foreword

1. Zhao Tingyang, 天下體系: 世界制度哲學導論 [The *tianxia* system: An introduction to the philosophy of world institution] (Beijing: People's Press, 2011), 1.

2. Sima Qian, *Shiji* [*Records of the Historian*] (Beijing: Zhonghua shuju, 1982): 淮阴侯列传 [Biography of Huaiyinhou]: 秦失其鹿, 天下共逐之.

3. A. C. Graham, *Studies in Chinese Philosophy and Philosophical Literature* (Albany: State University of New York Press, 1990), 360.

4. Tang Junyi, *Complete Works*, vol. 11 (Taipei: Xuesheng shuju, 1991), 16–17.

Introduction

1. "Historicity" is a core concept that originated with German and French historians and later came into common use in the philosophy of history and historiography. While there is agreement on the basic understanding and interpretation of the term, there are also differences. In this book I interpret historicity as including the general understanding of German and French scholars but also add an understanding based on a Chinese way of thinking.

2. [Translator's note: *D'où venons-nous? Que sommes-nous? Où allons-nous?* (1897), by Paul Gauguin, Museum of Fine Arts, Boston.]

3. Ludwig Wittgenstein, *Philosophical Investigations* (London: Macmillan, 1964), Question No. 309, "What is your aim in philosophy? To show the fly the way out of the fly-bottle."

4. Existence seeks to be forever. Although this is an inner demand of existence, pushed to an extreme it can turn into the opposite. To uphold the state of change of a state of existence, there is the judgment of Camus: "There is only one really serious philosophical question: suicide." And other

questions, "such as if the world has three dimensions, if the spirit has nine or twelve categories," or "whether the earth or the sun revolve around each other, is a matter of profound indifference." Cf. Albert Camus, *Le Mythe de Sisyphe* (1942), 1.1 *L'absurde et le suicide* (https://archive.org/stream/le_mythe_de_sisyphe/ mythe_de_sisyphe#page/n5/mode/2up [translator's note: my translation]. Suicide is an extreme example of acting against the basic meaning of existence, and therefore it is a real question. Camus's insight can be said to be profound, but for Camus to see it as the only question is a mistake because the meaning and force of the question of suicide is grounded in the meaning and force of the question of existence. In other words, that death can become a basic question is because life is a basic question. Shakespeare saw this more fully: "To be, or not to be; that is the question."

5. Cf. Thomas C. Schelling, *The Strategy of Conflict* (Cambridge, MA: Harvard University Press, 1981 [1960]), 48–51; Ken Binmore, *Game Theory: A Very Short Introduction* (Oxford: Oxford University Press, 2007), 58–60.

6. On the theory of universal models, see the introduction to my *Contemporaneity of* Tianxia: *Imagining and Realizing World Order* (Beijing: Zhongxin Press, 2016).

7. In my limited understanding, the simple concept of the earliest China was proposed by Xu Hong, but even before he had done so there were many other expressions and ways of speaking that came very close to it. In fact, we could say that China's archaeology and historicity have always sought the earliest China. [Editor's note: Xu Hong, *Zuizao de Zhongguo* (The earliest China) (Beijing: Science Press, 2009).]

8. The idea of a large, unified state comes from the *Gongyang* Commentary on the *Spring and Autumn Annals* (Duke Yin: Year One): " 'In the inaugural year, in spring, the king's first month.' What is the inaugural year? The year when the prince begins to rule. What is spring? The beginning of the year. Which king is being spoken of? King Wen. Why is mention first made of the king, and later of the first month? It is the king's first month. What is meant by 'the king's first month'? Great, unified rule." Great, unified rule originally applied to unification of the calendar. Affirming unification of the start of the calendar implies unification of political rule. Great, unified rule officially became a political concept with Dong Zhongshu (ca. 179-104 BCE). Dong Zhongshu said, "For Spring and Autumn to have great, unified rule is the constant norm of heaven and earth and the common custom of both past and present" (*Han History* 26 *Biography of Dong Zhongshu*). But such an explanation does not conform to the historical realities, since before the Qin and Han dynasties, the great, unified system of rule had not yet been discovered.

9. The idea of accompanying heaven is a basic principle of Chinese thought. It first appears in the *Book of History*: "When the rites of Yin held, [the kings] when dead accompanied Heaven" (*Book of History: Books of Zhou*

16 *Prince Shi*) and "The seasons accompanied August Heaven" (*Book of History: Books of Zhou 12 Announcement of the Duke of Shao*). Similar expressions occur elsewhere. "Combining its virtue with heaven and earth" (*Book of Changes: Qian Hexagram: Wen Yan Commentary*); "This is called accompanying heaven, the highest goal since ancient times" (*Daodejing* 68). The earliest detailed description is found in *The Mean and the Harmony*: "It is only the most sagely person in *tianxia*, who is intelligent and perspicacious, who suffices to approach it, and who is generous and gentle, who suffices to hold it, and who is strong and firm, who suffices to direct it, and who is set in the very center, who suffices to be respected, and who is well educated and discriminating, who suffices to set bounds for it. Vast and as deep as a spring, he is one who acts according to the seasons. Vast like heaven, a deep spring like an abyss: when seen, none of the people do not respect him; when he speaks none of the people do not trust him; when he acts none of the people do not rejoice in him. Therefore, his renown spreads throughout China and extends to the barbarians. Wherever boats or carriages get to, wherever human strength reaches, wherever heaven covers or earth upholds, wherever sun and moon shine, wherever frost or dew fall, none of those who have blood and *qi* do not respect and love him, therefore it is said, 'He accompanies heaven'" (*Book of Rites: The Mean and the Harmony* 32). It is also said: "Extensive and solid so as to accompany earth; high and bright to accompany heaven, lasting forever, without limit" (*Book of Rites: The Mean and the Harmony* 26).

10. "This is called accompanying heaven, the highest goal since ancient times" (*Daodejing* 68).

11. *Mencius* 7B25.

12. The current understanding of *zongjiao* 宗教 is the belief that takes the concept of religion as its norm. This is very far removed from the Chinese words *zong* 宗 (ancestral) and *jiao* 教 (teaching). Religion is a contractual agreement between humans and God, by which human beings accept the holy covenant of God and obey the guidance of God.

Chapter One: A Whirlpool Model of China

1. Previously, there have been some historians who have copied Western historical ideas and described Chinese society from the Qin to the Qing as a feudal dictatorship. This is a mistaken application of the term. The Zhou had a feudal system; from the Qin onward there were commanderies and counties. Nowadays, most people no longer use that erroneous expression, preferring instead Western political terms: a central despotism, or despotic political system of government, or the like. This way of speaking is partly correct but is not very accurate. Although the emperor was at the pinnacle of power in the imperial

dynasties from the Qin on, yet the old form of power sharing was still retained in part. Apart from the case of violent emperors who cared little for structure, the emperor could not normally rule alone. The Qin and Han set up various levels of consultative governance. Generally, the cabinet met in the imperial council to pass matters pertaining to state affairs. When an affair was particularly important or posed special difficulties, then it was necessary to invite all the officials of the central administration to take part in a meeting of the "hundred officials." Finally, the emperor would express his approval. Although each era had its own system, the basic principles remained the same. Yu Yingshi has shown that power sharing was at its best under the Song. Therefore, it is difficult to describe the Chinese polity as despotic, but to call it participatory would also be an exaggeration since in the final analysis the emperor held the power of veto. Since contemporary political studies lacks a term that can accurately describe China's dynastic past, it can provisionally be called an "executive unified rule." The main reason for this choice of expression is that the most important political structure under the Chinese dynasties was the distinction between the officials and the people—that is, the relationship between the bureaucracy and popular society—with the emperor ruling through the bureaucracy. Hence, it can be called an "executive unified rule."

2. The *tianxia* system seeks a politics of compatibility, a "compatibility of the many states" (*Book of History*). Compatibility implies that enemies can be transformed into friends and that acceptance can be used to guarantee peace at a political level.

3. *Sayings of the States: Sayings of Zhou A.*

4. The warlike King Mu made war on the Quan and Rong for their failure to present tribute on time. Although he won a great victory over them, he broke the harmony that had existed under the Zhou dynasty with the result that he lost the hearts of the Quan and Rong who no longer came to present any tribute at court.

5. *Record of Rites* 7: *Ceremonial Usages.*

6. Chen Mengjia, "Shangdai de shenhua yu wushu" [Legends and shamanism in the Shang era], *Yanjing Xuebao* 20 (1936).

7. Zhang Guangzhi, *Meishu: shenhua yu jisi* [Aesthetics: Legends and rituals] (Beijing: SDX Joint Publishing, 2013), 85.

8. Li Zehou, *You wu dao li: Shi li gui ren* [From the shaman to the rites: An interpretation of rites reverting to benevolence] (Beijing: SDX Joint Publishing, 2015), 13–21.

9. Zhang Xuecheng, Wang Yangming, Li Ao, and others already held the view that the six classics were all history, but Zhang Xuecheng expounds upon it in the greatest detail. See Zhang Xuecheng, *Wenshi tongyi*, vol. 1: *Yijiao A* [The synoptic meaning of literature and history: Teachings on the *Changes* A] (Shanghai: Shanghai guji Press, 2008), 1.

10. On this question of world politics, see the analysis in my *Tianxia de dangdaixing: Shijiezhixu de shixian yu xiangxiang* [The contemporaneity of *tianxia*: Imagining and realizing a world order] (Beijing: Zhongxin Press, 2016).

11. The surface similarities between ancient China and empires give rise to misinterpretation. I used to refer to ancient China as an empire, but later I corrected myself.

12. Tan Qixiang points out, "The Qing dynasty's use of troops against Mongolia cannot be considered militarism, just as the use by Emperor Wu of the Han of troops against the Xiongnu cannot be considered as such. Emperor Wu's treatment of Korea and the Eastern and Southern Yue may be regarded as invasions, but not so for his action against the Xiongnu. If he had not faced the Xiongnu, they would have fought their way in. The treatment of the Tujue (Turkic tribes) by the Taizong Emperor of the Tang cannot be considered militarism, any more than the Qing's treatment of the Uyghurs. See Tan Qixiang, "Tangdai jimizhou shulun" [A discussion of loose-rein prefectures in the Tang dynasty], in *Changshui cuibian* (Shijiazhuang: Hebei jiaoyu chubanshe, 2000), 7.

13. In earlier writings, I used the term "great power," but Lü Xiang suggested I use "leading power," because "great power" in contemporary political discourse is considered somewhat derogatory, with the implication of being overbearing. I follow his correction here.

14. Western sinologists Joseph Levenson and Lucien Pye hold that China was a civilization-state. An earlier proponent of this was Marcel Granet. Although he did not use the term itself, his famous book *La Civilization chinoise* (1929) analyzed Chinese society in terms of a civilization. Contemporary Confucians share a similar understanding. Qian Mu thought that China's "nation and state only existed for the sake of the civilization." Qian Mu, *Zhongguo wenhuashi daolun* [A guide to the cultural history of China] (Beijing: Commercial Press, 1994 [1948]), 23. Liang Shuming, however, thought "China succeeded in replacing the state by a society," *Zhongguo xiandai xueshu jingdian: Liang Shuming juan* [Contemporary Chinese scholarly classics: Liang Shuming] (Shijiazhuang: Hebei Education Press, 1996 [1949]), 520). Liang Shuming quotes a letter from a friend saying that when Bertrand Russell came to China in 1920, he noted in a conference in Shanghai, "China is indeed a civilization and not a nation-state" (255). From this it would seem that the earliest person to describe China as a civilization was Russell.

15. Wang Mingming, "Zhongguo: Minzuti haishi wenmingti?" [China: A national body or a civilization body?], *Wenhua zongheng* 12 (2008).

16. Many states in the Middle East, South America, and Africa can only be called nation-states with difficulty. In some cases, a nation of one people and one culture form certain states; while in others, different nations and different religions are included in the same state.

17. In 1901 Liang Qichao proposed nationalism. See Liang Qichao, "Guo-jia sixiang bianqian yitonglun" [A discussion of the change to thinking about nationalism], in *Yinbingshi heji* [Collected works of the Icedrinker's Studio], vol. 1, *wenji*, 6 (Beijing: Zhonghua shuju new edition, 1989). In 1902 he suggested the nation-state. "Lun minzu jingzheng zhi dashi" [On the important business of competition among nations], in *Yinbingshi heji* [Collected works of the Iced-rinker's Studio], vol. 2, *wenji*, 10 (Beijing: Zhonghua shuju new edition, 1989). But later he reverted to statism.

18. Popular proverbs reflect actual social realities better than moral teachings. Li Qingshan, in his *Zhongguo xinlun: cong minyan kan minxin* [A new discussion of China: Looking at the mind of the people from popular proverbs] (Beijing: Chinese Academy of Social Sciences, 1996), uses many contradictory proverbs to illustrate how there are two sides to much behavior, for instance, on the one hand, a desire to encourage upright, unselfish behavior and, on the other, to wriggle out of difficulties and seek one's best interest.

19. *Book of Changes: Great Appendix* A: "Daily renewal names growing in virtue; generation and regeneration name the Changes."

20. Eric Voegelin, *Order and History*, vol. 1: *Israel and Revelation* (Baton Rouge: Louisiana State University Press, 1956), 19.

21. Thomas C. Schelling, *The Strategy of Conflict*, Chinese ed. (Cambridge, MA: Harvard University Press, 2011), 48–51.

22. Zhang Guangzhi, *Gudai Zhongguo kaoguxue* [The archaeology of ancient China] (Beijing: SDX Joint Publishing, 2013), 434.

23. Su Bingqi, "Guanyu Taosi fajue baogao bianxie ji youguan wenti," in *Su Bingqi wenji* [Collected works of Su Bingqi], vol. 3 (Beijing: Cultural Relics Press, 2009), 15. The examples given by Su Bingqi are as follows: "Hongshan culture is not a variant of Yangshao culture; the lower stratum of Xiajiadian culture is not a variant of the Longshan culture of the Central Plain." One proof is that the bronze culture of the north and that of the Central Plain each have features that do not depend on the other.

24. Sima Qian, *Records of the Historian*, vol. 1: *Chronicles of the Five Emperors*.

25. Sima Qian, *Records of the Historian*, vol. 1: *Chronicles of the Five Emperors*: The Yellow Emperor "moved around and had no fixed abode relying on his troops to protect his camp." It can be seen that the Yellow Emperor was the leader of a nomadic tribe. This also explains why at least some nomadic tribes originally lived along the course of the Yellow River. The area over which the Yellow Emperor roamed stretched from Mongolia in the north to Shaanxi and Gansu in the west. So it may be that he belonged to the tribe later known as the Northern Di, or it could also have been the Western Rong.

26. Since this story is very ancient, there is no clear record. It may be that the battles at Banquan and at Zhuolu were not two battles but two stages in one battle. It is even the case that there is no definite conclusion regarding

the relationships between the Yellow Emperor, the Fiery Emperor, and Chi You. But it must be true that there was a war that led to the "stag hunt" on the Central Plain model.

27. In early China people were few and wild animals many, so hunting was the common form of life for the peoples in the four surrounding areas. The yields produced by early agriculturists and nomads were low so these forms of life could not have formed the only means of subsistence. Plowing by oxen is necessary for high agricultural yields. This technology dates to the Spring and Autumn and Warring States periods, but it was only widespread in the Han. High yields in pastoral life require the riding of horses. The collective model of horse-riding archers is not earlier than the Spring and Autumn era because King Wuling of Zhao only heard about the advantages of the northern dress and horse archers in the Warring States era. Cf. Xu Zhongshu, *Guqiwu zhong de gudai wenhua zhidu* [The ancient cultural institutions of ancient vessels] (Beijing: Commercial Press, 2015), 1–124, 374–80.

28. *Analects* 13.16.

29. Zhao Hui, "Yi zhongyuan wei zhongxin de lishi qushi de xingcheng" [The formation of the historical tendency that took the Central Plain as the center], *Wenwu* 1 (2000).

30. Zhang Guangzhi, *Kaoguxue zhuanti liu jiang* [Six lectures on archaeology] (Beijing: SDX Joint Publishing, 2013), 156.

31. A view that is still tentative holds that in early China there was, as well as Chinese characters, the ancient Yi script. But accounts are not clear, and it would seem the Yi script was not so well developed. It is said that the ancient Yi script was the old form of writing of the southwestern tribes and bore a definite relationship to today's Yi script. Extant texts in the Yi script are mostly from the Ming and Qing dynasties and have largely to do with prognostication that would seem to imply an earlier origin. Yet at what time the Yi script appeared and how mature it was and whether it could express complex abstract thought are all questions that await further research.

32. Christianity is also a successful example of transforming a particular into something universal. The passion and resurrection of Jesus is a particular narrative but proclaims a universal faith that is open to all.

Chapter Two: The China That Contains *Tianxia*

1. The popular view in Europe and America is that Sumerian civilization was much earlier than those of China and India, though this view is not unquestionable. Archaeological discoveries of the past decade indicate traces of civilization in China that are contemporary with that of the Sumerians, with early agriculture and crude pottery, but seemingly not so advanced as that of

Sumerians, though this awaits the discovery of further evidence. Here I keep to the popular view.

2. There are some indications that ancient China may have acquired certain skills from the ancient Middle East or from the western steppes, including bronze, but this is as yet unconfirmed. However, it is at least credible that some agricultural crops such as wheat came from the Middle East.

3. Yuan Jing, *Zhongguo dongwu kaoguxue* [Chinese animal archaeology] (Beijing: Cultural Relics Press, 2015),140–43; 179.

4. Zhongguo shehui kexueyuan kaogu yanjiusuo [Archaeological Institute, Chinese Academy of Social Sciences], *Zhongguo kaoguxue: xinshiqi shidai juan* [Chinese archaeology: Vol. Neolithic era] (Beijing: Chinese Academy of Social Science Press, 2010), 198–202.

5. Zhongguo shehui kexueyuan kaogu yanjiusuo, *Zhongguo kaoguxue*, 568.

6. Zhongguo shehui kexueyuan kaogu yanjiusuo, *Zhongguo kaoguxue*, 786–95.

7. Su Bingqi, "Guanyu Taosi fajue baogao bianxie ji youguan wenti," 14–15.

8. Zhang Guangzhi, *Zhongguo kaoguxue lunwenji* [Anthology of articles on Chinese archaeology] (Beijing: SDX Joint Publishing, 1999), 54–55.

9. Xu Hong, *Zuizao de Zhongguo*, 152.

10. Zhang Guangzhi, *Zhongguo kaoguxue lunwenji*, 36.

11. Zhang Guangzhi, *Zhongguo kaoguxue lunwenji*, 158–59.

12. Zhongguo shehui kexueyuan kaogu yanjiusuo, *Zhongguo kaoguxue*, 81.

13. Zhang Guangzhi believes that Erlitou culture looks as if it must be Xia culture, but the reason why he cannot quite decide if it is Xia or Shang culture is because "up to now no written material has been found in Erlitou culture." Zhang Guangzhi, *Gudai Zhongguo kaoguxue*, 376–77. The problem is that, based on current evidence, writing had not yet begun in the time of Erlitou and so the hope of finding any "written material" as proof is not great.

14. Liu Qingzhu, ed., *Zhongguo kaogu faxian yu yanjiu* (1949–2009) [Chinese archaeological discoveries and research (1949–2009)] (Beijing: People's Press, 2010), 196.

15. Xu Hong, *Heyi Zhongguo* [Whence China?] (Beijing: SDX Joint Publishing, 2014), 117–19.

16. The domestication of animals is a secondary indication of agriculture. The proportions of meat consumed at Erlitou were as follows: (first period) domestic 67 percent, wild 33 percent; (second period) domestic 75 percent, wild 25 percent; (third period) domestic 67 percent, wild 33 percent; (fourth period) domestic 87 percent, wild 13 percent. See Yuan Jing, *Zhongguo dongwu kaoguxue*, 141.

17. Zhongguo shehui kexueyuan kaogu yanjiusuo, *Zhongguo kaoguxue*, 107–23.

18. Xu Hong, *Heyi Zhongguo*, 107–23.

19. Xu Hong, *Heyi Zhongguo*, 146–47.

20. Zhang Guangzhi, *Gudai Zhongguo kaoguxue*, 346.

21. *Book of History: Zhou Books: Many Officials.*

22. Zhongguo shehui kexueyuan kaogu yanjiusuo, *Zhongguo kaoguxue*, 125.

23. Chen Mengjia, *Zhongguo wenzi xue* [A study of China's script] (Beijing: Zhonghua shuju, 2011), 11.

24. Xu Hong holds that while the palace at Erlitou is only one-seventh of the area of the Forbidden City, yet its format indicates that it was the forerunner of later Chinese imperial palaces. See Xu Hong, *Zuizao de Zhongguo*, 80–84.

25. *Rites of Zhou: Offices of Earth: Great Situ.*

26. *Shiji (Records of the Historian): Zhou benji: Zhou.*

27. Liang Sicheng, *Zhongguo jianzhushi* [A history of Chinese architecture] (Tianjin: Baihua wenyi Press, 1998), 15.

28. Yang Kuan, *Zhongguo gudai ducheng zhidu shi* [A history of ancient China's urban organization] (Shanghai: Shanghai People's Press, 2006), 25–36.

29. Nassim Nicholas Taleb, *Antifragile: Things That Gain from Disorder* (New York: Random House, 2012), 3.

30. For example, what is described as traditional dress today is Manchu dress. Many traditional musical instruments have come from the western reaches. Many of the songs that were proper to each people have become famous songs for all the peoples. In culinary matters, there is a great synthesis of east and west, south and north, and likewise in other matters.

31. Yao Dali, *Meng-Yuan zhidu yu zhengzhi wenhua* [The Mongolian Yuan dynasty organization and political culture] (Beijing: Peking University Press, 2011), 270.

32. Xu Pingfang, *Zhongguo chengshi kaoguxue lunji* [Collected essays on the archaeology of Chinese towns] (Shanghai: Shanghai guji, 2015), 81.

33. The information in this section on the Liao dynasty is all derived from Wang Ke, *Minzu yu guojia: Zhongguo duo minzu tongyi guojia sixiang xipu* [Nation and state: A genealogy of national state thought for the unification of China's many peoples] (Beijing: Chinese Academy of Social Sciences, 2001), 119–28.

34. Ge Zhaoguang, *Zhaizi zhongguo* [Living in this China] (Beijing: Zhonghua shuju, 2011), 41–42.

35. Quoted in Jao Tsung-i, *Zhongguo shixueshang zhi zhengtonglun* [Discussions of orthodoxy in Chinese history] (Beijing: Zhonghua shuju, 2015), 157–61.

36. Chen Gaohua and Shi Weimin, *Zhongguo zhengzhi zhidu tongshi* [A history of China's political institutions, vol. 8], ed. Bai Gang (Beijing: People's Press, 1996), 60.

37. Chen Gaohua and Shi Weimin, *Zhongguo zhengzhi zhidu tongshi*, 37–38.

38. Zhang Zhaoyu, "Mingdai hua-yi zhi bian" [The distinction between the Chinese and the barbarians in the Ming dynasty], in *Gushi wencun: Ming-*

Qing juanshang [Surviving ancient historical documents: Ming-Qing, vol. 1], ed. the Institute of History, Chinese Academy of Social Sciences (Beijing: Social Sciences Documentation Press, 2004), 265–77.

39. Qu Shigu, *Zhifangwaijixiaoyan* [Notes on Record of Foreign Lands], in *Zhifangwaijijiaoshi* [Annotated translation of Record of Foreign Lands] (Beijing: Zhonghua shuju, 2000), 9.

40. *Yuan History*, vol. 161: *Biography* 48.

41. *Xunzi: Kings and Hegemons.*

42. Jao Tsung-i, *Zhongguo shixueshang zhi zhengtonglun*, 6.

43. Ouyang Xiu, "Zhengtonglun shang" [A discussion of orthodox rule, part A], quoted in Jao Tsung-i, *Zhongguo shixueshang zhi zhengtonglun* [Discussions of orthodoxy in Chinese history] (Beijing: Zhonghua shuju, 2015), 114.

44. Sima Guang, *Zizhi tongjian* [A mirror for the wise ruler], vol. 69, *Wei Chronicles 1 Huang Year 2* (Shanghai: Shanghai guji, 1997).

45. Wang Fuzhi, *Songlun* [Commentary on the Song dynasty], in *Complete Works*, vol. 15 (Changxia: Yuelu Publishing House, 1991).

46. Gu Yanwu, *Rizhilu*, vol. 13 *Sikuquanshu* (1773), Chinese Text Project digital library.

47. Western historians often use the phrase "dynasties of conquest" to describe barbarians who invade civilized areas and set up kingdoms. Karl Wittfogel uses this term to refer to the northern people of China who entered the Central Plain and established dynasties (cf. Karl A. Wittfogel and Feng Chia-sheng, *History of Chinese Society: Liao, 907–1125* [Philadelphia: American Philosophical Society, 1949]). The general introduction to the 1961 Lancaster Press edition of this book argues that these peoples were not sinicized. Rather they shared their culture with the Han and the Han with them while retaining their hold on power of their own people. ("Acculturation'" is often translated by *hanhua*, which is not clear since it simply implies adapting to a new cultural environment.) Wittfogel's hypothesis is largely correct but his premise is wrong. He uses the Western nation-state as the basis for his understanding of China and hence arrives at the opinion expressed. But the problem is that China was originally formed by the common efforts of many cultures and peoples. Without the northern peoples, China could not have been formed and so one cannot classify some of the founding peoples of China as foreigners. Su Bingqi already pointed out that "China was formed jointly by the northern cultures, including the Laoha River and Daling River basin west of the Liao River in the northeast, and the culture of the Central Plain along the Yellow River and Fen River basin and the northern culture from Mongolia and the Daqing Mountains. This led to a 'Y-shaped' cultural root system." See Su Bingqi, *Su Bingqi wenji*, vol. 3, 47–54.

48. *Qing ruguanqian shiliao xuanji 1* [Selected historical documents from before the Qing came to the throne, vol. 1] (Beijing: People's Press, 1984), 289–96.

49. [Translator's note: For a discussion of this text, see Jonathan Spence, *Treason by the Book* (Harmondsworth, Middlesex: Penguin, 2002).]

50. John King Fairbank, ed., *The Chinese World Order: Traditional China's Foreign Relations* (Cambridge, MA: Harvard University Press, 1968), 283.

51. John King Fairbank, *The Chinese World Order*, 1.

52. Zheng Youguo, *Zhongguo shibo zhidu yanjiu* [A study of China's maritime customs] (Fuzhou: Fujian Education Press, 2004), 214–20.

53. Li Yunquan, *Wanbang laichao: chaogong zhidu shilun* [The many states come to court: A historical discussion of the institution of tribute] (Beijing: Xinhua Press, 2014), 13.

54. Yan Mingshu, *Zhongguo gudai heqin shi* [A history of China's ancient dynastic marriage] (Guiyang: Guizhou Nationalities Press, 2003), 157.

55. Shao Yiping, "Riben wenxianli de zhongguo" [China in Japanese documents], in *Yuwai wenxianli de Zhongguo* [China in foreign documents], ed. Fudan University Institute for Ancient Texts (Shanghai: Shanghai Wenyi Press, 2014), 130.

Chapter Three: The Game of "Stag Hunting" and the China Temptation

1. Sima Qian, *Records of the Historian: Biographies of the Marquises of Huaiyin*; see also Ban Gu, *Han History: Biography of Kuai Tong*.

2. Man Zhimin, *Zhongguo lishi shiqi qihou bianhua yanjiu* [Research into climate change in China's historical era] (Jinan: Shandong Education Press, 2009), 92–118.

3. The *Yi Zhoushu: Shi fu jie* (*Lost Book of Zhou*) records one major hunt undertaken by King Wu of Zhou: "King Wu went hunting and caught 22 tigers, 2 cats, 5,235 Père David's deer, 12 rhinoceroses, 721 yaks, 151 bears, 108 brown bears, 352 wild boar, 18 raccoon dogs, 16 mouse deer, 50 musk deer, 30 water deer, 3,508 deer." Altogether the number of deer of various species caught was 8,839 animals compared to 1,396 for all the other animals. This shows the vast difference in numbers.

4. Zhang Guangzhi, *Zhongguo kaoguxue lunwenji*, 53.

5. *Book of Changes* 3 Zhun Hexagram Line 3.

6. Xu Hong, *Heyi Zhongguo*, 96–99. See also Zhao Hui, "Yi zhongyuan wei zhongxin de lishi qushi de xingcheng."

7. Wang Wei, "Handai yiqian de sichou zhi lu" [The Silk Road in pre-Han times], *Journal of the Chinese Academy of Social Sciences* 12 (January 2016): 4. Also, according to Lin Meicun, silk with a phoenix pattern that came from the Central Plain, and dating from the Warring States period, has been discovered

in the Altai Mountains. Among artifacts from the Roman Empire, there are also pieces of Han dynasty silk. See *Sizhou zhi lu kaogu shiwu jiang* [Fifteen lectures on the archaeology of the Silk Road] (Beijing: Peking University Press, 2006), 8.

8. [Translator's note: Yugu is in Ningxia; Khotan in Xinjiang. See Denis Twitchett and Michael Loewe, *The Cambridge History of China*, vol. 1: *The Ch'in and Han Empires 221 BC–AD 220* (Cambridge: Cambridge University Press, 1986), 423.]

9. Yang Boda, *Zhongguo yuqi quanji* [Complete collection of Chinese jade artifacts], vol. 1 (Shijiazhuang: Hebei Arts Press, 2005), 5–16.

10. See Mancur Olsen, *Power and Prosperity: Outgrowing Communist and Capitalist Dictatorships* (Oxford: Oxford University Press, 2000); *The Rise and Decline of Nations: Economic Growth, Stagflation, and Social Rigidities* (New Haven: Yale University Press, 1982); *The Logic of Collective Action: Public Goods and the Theory of Groups* (Cambridge, MA: Harvard University Press, 1965).

11. Alfred Gell, "The Technology of Enchantment and the Enchantment of Technology," *Ethnic Arts Quarterly* 3 (2015). Gell explains that in today's life the technology of enchantment continues to exist in such things as advertising, marketing, and visual design.

12. The sage king Zhuan Xu prevented the folk religious practice of communicating with the spirits and put an end to folk shamans communicating with heavenly spirits. See my *Tianxia: tout sous un même ciel* (Paris: Éditions du Cerf, 2018), 108–09.

13. Liang Shuming, *Zhongguo wenhua yaoyi* [les Idées maîtresses de la culture chinoise], trans. Michel Masson (Paris: Éditions du Cerf, 2010), 379. Liang Qichao referred to the advantage of the universality of Chinese characters even earlier. Liang Qichao, "Zhongguo lishishang minzu zhi yanjiu" [Historical research into the Chinese nation], in *Yinbingshi heji* [Collected works of the Icedrinker's Studio], vol. 1, *wenji* 42 (Beijing: Zhonghua shuju new edition, 1989). Here Liang Shuming expands and develops Liang Qichao's ideas.

14. *Book of Changes: Great Appendix* A12.

15. *Book of History 5 Books of Zhou 17 Mandate to Zhong of Cai.*

16. *Book of History 5 Books of Shang 6 Both Possessed Pure Virtue 3.*

17. Zhou Zhenhe, *Zhongguo lishi zhengzhi dili 16 jiang* [16 lectures on Chinese historical-political geography] (Beijing: Zhonghua shuju, 2013), 256.

18. *Debates on Salt and Iron 38 Preparing to Deal with the Hu.*

19. *Debates on Salt and Iron 46 The Western Regions.*

20. *Debates on Salt and Iron 45 Punishing Aggression.*

21. Li Hongbin, "Zhulu zhongyuan: Dongbei zhuzu nanxiang kuozhande mimi" [Stag hunting on the Central Plain: The secret of the expansion of the northeastern tribes toward the south], *Bulletin of the Chinese Academy of Social Sciences* 29 (January 2015).

22. *Record of Rites 1 Summary of the Rites.*

23. Jia Yi, *New Book: Xiongnu.*

24. Ban Gu, *Han History* 96B *History of the Western Region.*

25. Ban Gu, *Han History* 70 *Biography of Zheng Ji.*

26. Meng Xiangcai, *Zhongguo zhengzhi zhidu tongshi* [A history of China's political organization], vol. 3, ed. Bai Gang (Beijing: People's Press, 1996), 257–58.

27. The loose-rein prefecture was an institution used by the imperial court to control the frontiers in a manner adapted to the topography. It differed in details according to time and place. Its basic principle was to grant autonomy to areas controlled by the central government. Troops were generally sent to manage key points. However, they did not interfere in the traditional ways of life or organization. Du You (735–812) said, "Virtue goes far; the barbarians of the four quarters are transformed by it. Govern for the sake of human beings and do not seek to satisfy your own desires. This is what the loose-rein prefecture is." Du You, *Tong Dian* [Historical encyclopedia], vol. 171: *Zhoujundian xu* [Preface to the section on Zhou commandery (801 AD)] (Beijing: Zhonghua shuju, 1988).

28. Huang Huixian, *Zhongguo zhengzhi zhidu tongshi* [A history of Chinese political institutions, vol. 4], ed. Bai Gang (Beijing: People's Press, 1996), 72–80.

29. Sima Guang, *Zizhi tongjian* [A mirror for the wise ruler], vol. 198: *Tang Annals* 14 *Zhenguan Year* 21 (Shanghai: Shanghai guji, 1997).

30. Yu Lunian, *Zhongguo zhengzhi zhidu tongshi* [A history of Chinese political institutions], vol. 5 (Beijing: People's Press, 1996), 256–60.

31. Tan Qixiang, "Tangdai jimizhou shulun," 150–61.

32. Li Xihou and Bai Bin, *Zhongguo zhengzhi zhidu tongshi* [A history of Chinese political institutions, vol. 7] (Beijing: People's Press, 1996), 2, 74–87.

33. Wang Tongling, *Zhongguo minzushi* [A history of China's nationalities] (Changchun: Jilin Publishing Group, 2010), 394–98.

34. Yao Dali, *Meng-Yuan zhidu yu zhengzhi wenhua*, 280.

35. Yao Dali, *Meng-Yuan zhidu yu zhengzhi wenhua*, 280.

36. Sima Qian, *Records of the Historian*, vol. 1: *Genealogy of the Five Emperors.*

37. Wang Tongling, *Zhongguo minzushi*, 18–28.

38. Wang Tongling, *Zhongguo minzushi*, preface.

39. *Zhenguan zhengyao: Pacifying the Frontiers*: "Following the defeat of the Turk Xieli (Illig Qaghan), many tribal leaders came to surrender and all acknowledged the general commander of the palace guard and served at court. There were over a hundred made mandarins of the fifth rank and above, virtually equivalent to the courtiers."

40. Wang Tongling, *Zhongguo minzushi*, 335–525.

41. Wang Tongling, *Zhongguo minzushi*, 440–41.

42. Gongsun Long: *Discourse on Indicating Things.* [Translator's note: See A. C. Graham, *Disputers of the Tao* (La Salle, IL: Open Court, 1989), 92ff.]

43. Gongsun Long, *Discourse on Indicating Things.* [Translator's note: See A. C. Graham, *Disputers of the Tao*, 93.]

44. [Translator's note: Quoting the *Great Appendix* to the *Book of Changes*. The expression "what is above form" is employed as the standard translation of the Greek word "metaphysics."]

45. *Wei History*, vol. 1: *Preface*.

46. Su Bingqi pointed out much earlier, "To take the Great Wall as a state border is utterly incompatible with historical truth." It is a "false distortion." See Su Bingqi, *Collected Writings of Su Bingqi*, vol. 2, 286.

47. Duan Qingbo and Xu Weimin, *Zhongguo lidai changcheng: faxian yu yanjiu* [China's historic great walls: Discovery and research] (Beijing: Science Press, 2014), 1–17.

48. Duan Qingbo and Xu Weimin, *Zhongguo lidai changcheng: faxian yu yanjiu*, 114–56.

49. Duan Qingbo and Xu Weimin, *Zhongguo lidai changcheng: faxian yu yanjiu*, 247–48.

50. Duan Qingbo and Xu Weimin, *Zhongguo lidai changcheng: faxian yu yanjiu*, 284–85.

51. Duan Qingbo and Xu Weimin, *Zhongguo lidai changcheng: faxian yu yanjiu*, 304.

52. Zhou Zhenhe, *Zhongguo lishi zhengzhi dili 16 jiang*, 75–77.

53. Fu Sinian, *Minzu yu gudai zhongguo shi* [Nation and ancient China's history] (Shijiazhuang: Hebei Educational Press, 2002), 3.

54. Su Bingqi, *Collected Writings of Su Bingqi*, vol. 2, 271.

Chapter Four: Method and Destiny

1. "Robustness" is normally interpreted as an unclearly defined obtuseness. A more accurate sense is a thick-skinned or an especially hardy ability that can ride safely through adversity.

2. According to analytic philosophy, these metaphysical beliefs lack truth value; that is, they can neither be proved nor disproved. Early on, analytic philosophy held that beliefs that lack truth value should not be believed and should be set aside. Later it was discovered that many beliefs lacking in truth value are in fact the basic ideas upon which human thought must depend. It is for this reason that metaphysics has made a comeback.

3. *Book of Changes: Great Appendix* A.

4. *Book of Changes: Great Appendix* B: "The great virtue of heaven and earth is called 'life.'"

5. *Book of Rites: The Mean and Harmony*.

6. *Book of Changes: Great Appendix* A11.

7. *Daodejing* 64.

8. *Record of Rites: The Mean and Harmony*: "Only a person who is most truly themselves can completely fulfill their nature. When a person can completely

fulfill their own nature, they can fulfill that of others. When they can fulfill the nature of others then they can fulfill the nature of things. When they can fulfill the nature of things then they can share in the transforming growth of heaven and earth. And when they can share in the transforming growth of heaven and earth, they can form a threesome with heaven and earth." The text continues, "What has integrity takes on form. What takes on form becomes visible. What is visible can be seen. What is seen can move. What moves can change. What changes can bring about change. Only that which has the utmost integrity in *tianxia* can bring about change."

9. *Daodejing* 8 and *Daodejing* 78: "There is nothing in *tianxia* weaker than water, yet in attacking what is firm and strong there is nothing that can overcome it. This is because there is nothing that can be used in its stead."

10. *Record of Rites: The Mean and Harmony.*

11. *Book of Changes: Great Appendix A:* "That which is above form is called the Way; that which are below form are called phenomena. Changing and tailoring things is called flux. Their application and putting them into practice is called continuity. To take up this understanding and bring it into the lives of the people of *tianxia* is called the grand undertaking."

12. Zhao Tingyang, *Diyi zhexue de zhidian* [The fulcrum of first philosophy] (Beijing: SDX Joint Publishing, 2013), 228. Here the normal interpretation of Descartes's axiom is used. In truth, a more correct reading would be "thinking therefore existing." Correspondingly, the axiom for Chinese thought ought to be "doing therefore existing." The Latin words *cogito* and *facio* include the self as part of the word and it is thus implicit, just as in ancient Chinese "think" and "do" also imply the subject.

13. *Daodejing* 59.

14. *Book of Changes: Great Appendix B.*

15. [Translator's note: The nodes recur at intervals of fifteen days. See John S. Major, *Heaven and Earth in Early Han Thought* (Albany: State University of New York Press, 1993), 88–90.]

16. *Analects* 8.8.

17. Han Linde, *Jingsheng xiangwai* [An aesthetic that transcends the physical object] (Beijing: SDX Joint Publishing, 1995), 192–248. Han holds that the layout and movements of all things in heaven and earth have a rhythm, and so the way of heaven itself is a great music. The five notes and twelve semitones correspond to the five agents, five directions, four seasons, and twelve months: "notes and calendar harmonize together." According to *Mr. Lü's Spring and Autumn Annals*, chap. 6: *The Patterns of Heaven*, the twelve semi-tones are fixed according to the respective winds of the twelve months. *Huainanzi*, chap. 3: *The Patterns of Heaven* also has a similar view.

18. *Record of Rites: Record of Music.*

19. Fei Xiaotong, *From the Soil: The Foundations of Chinese Society—A Translation of Fei Xiaotong's* Xiangtu zhongguo, trans. Gary G. Hamilton and

Wang Zheng (Berkeley: University of California Press, 1992 [original Chinese text: 1947]).

20. *Book of Changes: Explanation of the Trigrams.*

21. *Book of Changes: The Kun Hexagram: Tuan Definition.*

22. In his essay "On Mr. Rudyard Kipling and Making the World Small," Chesterton says: "The moment we are rooted in a place, the place vanishes. We live like a tree with the whole strength of the universe. . . . A cosmopolitan 'lacks altogether the faculty of attaching himself to any cause or community.' . . . The globetrotter lives in a smaller world than the peasant. He is always breathing an air of locality. . . . But Timbuctoo is not a place, since there, at least, live men who regard it as the universe, and breathe not an air of locality, but the winds of the world." Gilbert K. Chesterton, *Heretics* (London: John Lane, 1905), chap. 3. [Translator's note: The Chinese quotation abridges and reorders the text; the translation here follows the Chinese and not the original.]

23. *Book of Changes: Great Appendix B.*

24. [Translator's note: If the Middle County (China) is placed in the center of a grid of nine squares, the other eight are the eight wastelands. The six directions are north, south, east, west, up, and down.]

25. Han Linde, *Jingsheng xiangwai*, 108.

26. Han Linde, *Jingsheng xiangwai*, 107–08. Fan Xide provides several examples: a poem by Su Shi reads, "Gazing down on the Jiang and Han Rivers flowing by; looking up at the floating clouds flying by." Cao Pi's poem says, "Looking down on the green water waves; looking up at the bright moonlight." Xie Lingyun's poem says, "Looking down on the proud tree's twigs, gazing up at the great ravine's bubbling stream." Han Linde adds further examples: Song Yu's "Gazing on a mountain peak; looking down on the inaccessible places," Zhang Heng's "looking up at the arrow flying with a thread attached; looking down as the hook is borne along in the river," and Pan Gu's "Gazing insightfully on the spirit of the eastern well; bending down to assist the soul of the River Chart."

27. *Book of Rites: The Great Learning.*

28. Zhao Tingyang, *Diyi zhexue de zhidian*, 219. Zhao uses the term "creationology."

29. Jorge Luis Borges, "The Garden of Forking Paths" (*El jardín de senderos que se bifurcan*) (1941), English translation by Donald A. Yates with revisions by Seymour Menton from Jorge Luis Borges, *Labyrinths* (1962), in *The Spanish American Short Story: A Critical Anthology*, ed. Seymour Menton (Berkeley: University of California Press, 1980), 267.

30. Jorge Luis Borges, "The Garden of Forking Paths," 267.

31. See Ma Rusen, *Yinxu jiaguwen shiyong zidian* [A practical dictionary of the oracle bone script from the Yin ruins] (Shanghai: Shanghai University Press, 2014), 189 and 288. [Translator's note: Les Instituts Ricci, *Dictionnaire Ricci de caractères chinois* (Paris: Desclée de Brouwer, 1999), 20 no. 134.]

32. Xu Zhongshu, ed., *Jiaguwen zidian* [Dictionary of the oracle bone script] (Chengdu: Sichuan Dictionary Press, 2014), 888. [Translator's note: One side of the Chinese robe crosses the other at the neck. The character supposedly depicts this crossing.]

33. *Book of Changes: Great Appendix* B.

34. *Book of History* 1 *Canon of Yao* [cf. James Legge, trans., *The Chinese Classics* III: *The Shoo King* (London: Henry Frowde, Oxford University Press, 1865), 17–18.]

35. *Hanfeizi: Five Vermin*.

36. *Guanzi* 86 *Light and Heavy* V.

37. *Lushi Chunqiu: Shenfenlan: junshou*.

38. *Huainanzi: Benjing*.

39. *Shiben: Zuo pian:* Stories of Hereditary Families.

40. Qi Sihe, *Zhongguo shi tanyan* [A study of Chinese history] (Shijiazhuang: Hebei Educational Press, 2000), 389–414.

41. Zhang Xuecheng, *Wenshi tongyi*, 2: *Yuandao* A [The synoptic meaning of literature and history, vol. 2: The original way part 1] (Shanghai: Shanghai guji Press, 2008), 36–37. See Philip J. Ivanhoe, trans., *On Ethics and History: Essays and Letters of Zhang Xuechen* (Stanford: Stanford University Press, 2009).

42. Zhang Xuecheng, *Wenshi tongyi*, vol. 2, 36–37. See Philip J. Ivanhoe, *On Ethics and History*.

43. Zhang Xuecheng, says, "It is not the case that the Master (Confucius) honoring the first kings, out of a sense of humility did not himself create. Rather, it is that there was nothing which could be created. He had virtue but no post and so no authority to shape a new order." *Wenshi tongyi*, vol. 2, 37. See Philip J. Ivanhoe, *On Ethics and History*.

44. Sima Qian, *Records of the Historian* 130: *Authorial Preface by the Grand Astrologer*.

45. Zhang Wenjiang believes that there are two levels among the six classics. The *Book of Changes* and its appendices and the *Spring and Autumn Annals* are on one level. The *Book of Odes*, *Book of History*, *Record of Rites*, and *Record of Music* are on a lower level. Zhang Wenjiang, *Shiji taishigong zixu jiangji* [Notes on the Grand Astrologer's authorial preface to *Records of the Historian*] (Shanghai: Shanghai wenyi Press, 2015), 88. The reason for granting such prominence to the *Spring and Autumn Annals* must be due to the emphasis laid on Confucius's creative compilation. I fully support this judgment, but it might be better if the first level were to also include the *Book of History*. The *Book of History* represents the creation of the institutions of the Western Zhou. The *Spring and Autumn Annals* is the creation and compilation of Confucius. The *Book of Changes* and its appendices in terms of methodology brings together the creation of the three eras (Xia, Shang, Zhou). All are creations that have a universal methodological nature.

46. Zhang Xuecheng, *Wenshi tongyi*, vol. 2, 1. See Philip J. Ivanhoe, *On Ethics and History*.

47. *Record of Rites: The Great Treatise* 4–5: "When the sage faces south and regulates *tianxia*, he must begin from the way of humankind. Determining weights and measurements, decreeing the ceremonial, altering the beginning of the year and the months, changing the color of robes, differentiating flags and emblems, changing the vessels and weapons used, distinguishing types of shirt and dress to be worn—all of these are changed for the people. What cannot be changed is loving one's relatives, honoring the worthy, respecting the aged, and keeping a distinction between men and women. These latter may not be changed for the people."

48. For instance, in the *Spring and Autumn Annals*, the phrase "assassinated the prince" has the following implicit, logical significance: (1) There is the fact of a case of assassination of the ruler; also (2) a commonly held, unspoken norm has been destroyed. Since this norm is commonly held and unspoken, why should it need to be highlighted again? Because the person who destroyed the norm did not set out to destroy the social order but only to kill someone and reign in his stead. Hence by making this explicit and reminding people who hold this unspoken view—including the aggressor—the illegitimacy of the assassination is highlighted. There is no person who destroys the social order who would like anyone else to imitate what he has done. Clearly, the person who destroyed the norm sought to obtain power illegally.

49. Zhang Xuecheng, *Wenshi tongyi*, vol. 2, 1. See Philip J. Ivanhoe, *On Ethics and History*.

50. Xu Zhongshu, *Jiaguwen zidian*, 725.

51. [Translator's note: *Analects* 9.17.]

52. Xu Zhongshu, *Jiaguwen zidian*, 616.

53. Since Hume, empiricism holds that constantly repeated experience is not sufficient to guarantee that what will happen tomorrow will necessarily come to pass. For instance, the setting and rising of the sun is not an absolute necessity. In scientific terms, this understanding is correct. However, here I am discussing the conditions of life in which everything happens normally.

54. *Mozi: Against Aggression* B.

55. Feng Shi, *Zhongguo gudai de tianwen yu renwen* [Astronomy and human affairs in China's ancient past] (Beijing: Chinese Academy of Social Sciences, 2006), 9–13.

56. According to Ma Rusen, the things conveyed by the cross and the mouth are past things. See *Yinxu jiaguwen shiyong zidian*, 57.

57. Xu Zhongshu, *Jiaguwen zidian*, 574.

58. Cf. Alain Badiou, *Saint Paul: The Foundation of Universalism*, trans. Ray Brassier (Stanford: Stanford University Press, 2003).

59. For greater detail, see Zhou Dingyang, *Tianxia de dangdaixing* [The contemporaneity of *tianxia*] (Beijing: Zhongxin Press, 2016), chap. 1.

60. The term "sublimation" is a Hegelian concept that means rejecting the dross and keeping the good, and it is close to the idea of progress. While this appears to be reasonable, in fact it is confused and unclear. What is dross? What is good? By what standard? Whose standard? How should the standard be determined? And is there a standard for the standard?

61. Ancient views of history are often regressive or cyclical. In the chapter on "Ceremonial Usages" in the *Record of Rites*, there are regressive theories and the cyclical theory of the five virtues. Plato has a regressive theory, the Stoics a cyclical theory, and so on. I wonder if the ancients found regressive or cyclical theories to be a spontaneous way of looking at history, since it would seem to be a natural feeling that has not been thought about very much. However, the infinite changing historical outlook of the *Book of Changes* and the contemporary progressive theory are both the product of rational thought, and both have rational support.

62. As Edmund Burke points out, the revolutionaries of his time were guilty of "leaving a ruin instead of a habitation to those who come after them—and teaching these successors to respect their contrivances as little as *they* had respected the institutions of their forefathers." See Edmund Burke, *On the French Revolution*, part 2, section 8: "Caution in amending the state," www.earlymoderntexts.com/assets/pdfs/burke1790part2.pdf (consulted 11 July 2018).

Bibliography

Badiou, Alain. *Saint Paul: The Foundation of Universalism*. Translated by Ray Brassier. Stanford: Stanford University Press, 2003.

Binmore, Ken. *Game Theory: A Very Short Introduction*. Oxford: Oxford University Press, 2007.

Borges, Jorge Luis. "The Garden of Forking Paths" (*El jardín de senderos que se bifurcan*). English translation by Donald A. Yates with revisions by Seymour Menton from Jorge Luis Borges, *Labyrinths* (1962). In *The Spanish American Short Story: A Critical Anthology*, edited by Seymour Menton, 258–70. Berkeley: University of California Press, 1980.

Burke, Edmund. *On the French Revolution*, part 2, section 8: "Caution in amending the state." www.earlymoderntexts.com/assets/pdfs/burke1790part2.pdf (consulted 11 July 2018).

Camus, Albert. *Le Mythe de Sisyphe* (1942). 1.1 *L'absurde et le suicide*. https://archive.org/stream/le_mythe_de_sisyphe/mythe_de_sisyphe#page/n5/mode/2up.

Chang, K. C. *See* Zhang Guangzhi 张光直.

Chen, Gaohua 陈高华 and Shi Weimin 史卫民. *Zhongguo zhengzhi zhidu tongshi* 中国政治制度通史, 第八卷 [A history of China's political institutions], vol. 8. Edited by Bai Gang 白刚主编. Beijing: People's Press, 1996.

Chen, Mengjia 陈梦家. *Zhongguo wenzi xue* 中国文字学 [A study of China's script]. Beijing: Zhonghua shuju, 2011.

———. "Shangdai de shenhua yu wushu" 商代的神话与巫术 (Legends and shamanism in the Shang era]. *Yanjing Xuebao* 20 燕京学报 (1936).

Chesterton, Gilbert K. *Heretics*. London: John Lane, 1905.

Du, You 杜佑. *Tong Dian* 通典 [Historical encyclopedia], vol. 171: *Zhoujundian xu* 州郡典序 [Preface to the section on Zhou commandery (801 AD)]. Beijing: Zhonghua shuju, 1988.

Duan, Qingbo 段清波 and Xu Weimin 徐卫民. *Zhongguo lidai changcheng: faxian yu yanjiu* 中国历代长城: 发现与研究 [China's historic great walls: Discovery and research]. Beijing: Science Press, 2014.

Fairbank, John King, ed. *The Chinese World Order: Traditional China's Foreign Relations*. Cambridge, MA: Harvard University Press, 1968.

Fei, Xiaotong 费孝通. *From the Soil: The Foundations of Chinese Society—A Translation of Fei Xiaotong's* Xiangtu zhongguo. Translated by Gary G. Hamilton and Wang Zheng. Berkeley: University of California Press, 1992 [original Chinese text: 1947].

Feng, Shi 冯时. *Zhongguo gudai de tianwen yu renwen* 中国古代的天文与人文 [Astronomy and human affairs in China's ancient past]. Beijing: Chinese Academy of Social Sciences, 2006.

Fu, Sinian 傅斯年. *Minzu yu gudai zhongguo shi* 民族与古代中国史 [Nation and ancient China's history]. Shijiazhuang: Hebei Educational Press, 2002.

Ge, Zhaoguang 葛兆光. *Zhaizi zhongguo* 宅兹中国 [Living in this China]. Beijing: Zhonghua shuju, 2011.

Gell, Alfred. "The Technology of Enchantment and the Enchantment of Technology." *Ethnic Arts Quarterly* 3 (2015).

Graham, A. C. *Studies in Chinese Philosophy and Philosophical Literature*. Albany: State University of New York Press, 1990.

———. *Disputers of the Tao*. La Salle, IL: Open Court, 1989.

Gu, Yanwu 顾炎武. *Rizhilu* 日知录, vol. 13 *Sikuquanshu* 四库全书 (1773). Chinese Text Project digital library.

Han, Linde 韩林德. *Jingsheng xiangwai* 境生象外 [An aesthetic that transcends the physical object]. Beijing: SDX Joint Publishing, 1995.

Huang, Huixian 黄惠贤. *Zhongguo zhengzhi zhidu tongshi* 中国政治制度通史, 第四卷 [A history of Chinese political institutions], vol. 4. Edited by Bai Gang 白刚主编. Beijing: People's Press, 1996.

Ivanhoe, Philip J., trans. *On Ethics and History: Essays and Letters of Zhang Xuecheng*. Stanford: Stanford University Press, 2009.

Jao, Tsung-i 饶宗颐. *Zhongguo shixueshang zhi zhengtonglun* 中国史学上之正统论 [Discussions of orthodoxy in Chinese history]. Beijing: Zhonghua shuju, 2015.

Legge, James, trans. *The Chinese Classics III: The Shoo King*. London: Henry Frowde, Oxford University Press, 1865.

Les Instituts Ricci. *Dictionnaire Ricci de caractères chinois*. Paris: Desclée de Brouwer, 1999.

Li, Hongbin 李鸿宾. "Zhulu zhongyuan: Dongbei zhuzu nanxiang kuozhande mimi" 逐鹿中原: 东北诸族南向扩展的秘密 [Stag hunting on the Central Plain: The secret of the expansion of the northeastern tribes toward the south]. *Bulletin of the Chinese Academy of Social Sciences* 中国社会科学报 29 (January 2015).

Li, Qingshan 李庆善. *Zhongguo xinlun: cong minyan kan minxin* 中国新论: 从民谚看民心 [A new discussion of China: Looking at the mind of the people from popular proverbs]. Beijing: Chinese Academy of Social Sciences, 1996.

Li, Xihou 李锡厚 and Bai Bin 白滨. *Zhongguo zhengzhi zhidu tongshi* 中国政治制度通史, 第七卷 [A history of Chinese political institutions], vol. 7. Beijing: People's Press, 1996.

Li, Yunquan 李云泉. *Wanbang laichao: chaogong zhidu shilun* 万邦来朝: 朝贡制度史论 [The many states come to court: A historical discussion of the institution of tribute]. Beijing: Xinhua Press, 2014.

Li, Zehou 李泽厚. *You wu dao li: Shi li gui ren* 由巫到礼: 释礼归仁 [From the shaman to the rites: An interpretation of rites reverting to benevolence]. Beijing: SDX Joint Publishing, 2015.

Liang, Qichao 梁启超. "Guojia sixiang bianqian yitonglun" 国家思想变迁异同论 [A discussion of the change to thinking about nationalism]. In *Yinbingshi heji* 饮冰室合集 [Collected works of the Icedrinker's Studio], vol. 1, *wenji* 文集, 6, 1901. Beijing: Zhonghua shuju new edition, 1989.

———. "Lun minzu jingzheng zhi dashi" 论民族竞争之大势 [On the important business of competition among nations]. In *Yinbingshi heji* 饮冰室合集 [Collected works of the Icedrinker's Studio], vol. 2, *wenji* 文集, 10. Beijing: Zhonghua shuju new edition, 1989.

———. "Zhongguo lishishang minzu zhi yanjiu" 中国历史上民族之研究 [Historical research into the Chinese nation]. In *Yinbingshi heji* 饮冰室合集 [Collected works of the Icedrinker's Studio], vol. 1, *wenji* 文集, 42. Beijing: Zhonghua shuju new edition, 1989.

Liang, Shuming 梁漱溟. *Zhongguo wenhua yaoyi* 中国文化要义 [les Idées maîtresses de la culture chinoise]. Translated by Michel Masson. Paris: Éditions du Cerf, 2010.

———. *Zhongguo xiandai xueshu jingdian: Liang Shuming juan* 中国现代学术经典: 梁漱溟卷 [Contemporary Chinese scholarly classics: Liang Shuming]. Shijiazhuang: Hebei Education Press, 1996.

Liang, Sicheng 梁思成. *Zhongguo jianzhushi* 中国建筑史 [A history of Chinese architecture]. Tianjin: Baihua wenyi Press, 1998.

Lin, Meicun 林梅村. *Sizhou zhi lu kaogu shiwu jiang* 丝绸之路考古十五讲 [Fifteen lectures on the archaeology of the Silk Road]. Beijing: Peking University Press, 2006.

Liu, Qingzhu 刘庆柱主编, ed. *Zhongguo kaogu faxian yu yanjiu* 中国考古发现与研究 (1949–2009) [Chinese archaeological discoveries and research (1949–2009)]. Beijing: People's Press, 2010.

Ma, Rusen 马如森. *Yinxu jiaguwen shiyong zidian* 殷墟甲骨文实用字典 [A practical dictionary of the oracle bone script from the Yin ruins]. Shanghai: Shanghai University Press, 2014.

Major, John S. *Heaven and Earth in Early Han Thought*. Albany: State University of New York Press, 1993.

Man, Zhimin 满志敏. *Zhongguo lishi shiqi qihou bianhua yanjiu* 中国历史时期气候变化研究 [Research into climate change in China's historical era]. Jinan: Shandong Education Press, 2009.

Meng, Xiangcai 孟祥才. *Zhongguo zhengzhi zhidu tongshi* 中国政治制度通史第三卷 [A history of China's political organization, vol. 3]. Edited by Bai Gang 白刚主编. Beijing: People's Press, 1996.

Olsen, Mancur. *The Logic of Collective Action: Public Goods and the Theory of Groups*. Cambridge, MA: Harvard University Press, 1965.

———. *Power and Prosperity: Outgrowing Communist and Capitalist Dictatorships*. Oxford: Oxford University Press, 2000.

———. *The Rise and Decline of Nations: Economic Growth, Stagflation, and Social Rigidities*. New Haven: Yale University Press, 1982.

Ouyang, Xiu 欧阳修. "Zhengtonglun shang" 正统论上 [A discussion of orthodox rule, part A]. Quoted in Jao Tsung-i 饶宗颐, *Zhongguo shixueshang zhi zhengtonglun* 中国史学上之正统论 [Discussions of orthodoxy in Chinese history]. Beijing: Zhonghua shuju, 2015.

Qi, Sihe 齐思和. *Zhongguo shi tanyan* 中国史探研 [A study of Chinese history]. Shijiazhuang: Hebei Educational Press, 2000.

Qian, Mu 钱穆. *Zhongguo wenhuashi daolun* 中国文化史导论 [A guide to the cultural history of China]. Beijing: Commercial Press, 1994.

Qing ruguanqian shiliao xuanji 清入关前史料选辑 1 [Selected historical documents from before the Qing came to the throne, vol. 1]. Beijing: People's Press, 1984.

Qu, Shigu 瞿式穀. *Zhifangwaijixiaoyan* 职方外纪小言 [Notes on Record of Foreign Lands]. In *Zhifangwaijijiaoshi* 职方外纪校释 [Annotated translation of Record of Foreign Lands]. Beijing: Zhonghua shuju, 2000.

Rao, Congyi 饶宗颐. See Jao Tsung-i.

Schelling, Thomas C. *The Strategy of Conflict*. Cambridge, MA: Harvard University Press, 1981. Chinese translation 2011.

Shao, Yiping 邵毅平. "Riben wenxianli de zhongguo" 日本文献里的中国 [China in Japanese documents]. In *Yuwai wenxianli de Zhongguo* 域外文献里的中国 [China in foreign documents], edited by Fudan University Institute for Ancient Texts. Shanghai: Shanghai Wenyi Press, 2014.

Sima, Guang 司马光. *Zizhi tongjian* 资治通鉴 [A mirror for the wise ruler], vol. 69: *Wei Chronicles 1 Huang Year 2*. Shanghai: Shanghai guji, 1997.

———. *Zizhi tongjian* 资治通鉴 [A mirror for the wise ruler], vol. 198: *Tang Annals 14 Zhenguan Year 21*. Shanghai: Shanghai guji, 1997.

Sima, Qian 司马迁. *Shiji* 史记 (*Records of the Historian*). Beijing: Zhonghua shuju, 1982.

Sizhou zhi lu kaogu shiwu jiang [Fifteen lectures on the archaeology of the Silk Road]. Beijing: Peking University Press, 2006.

Spence, Jonathan. *Treason by the Book*. Harmondsworth, Middlesex: Penguin, 2002.

Su, Bingqi 苏秉琦. "Guanyu Taosi fajue baogao bianxie ji youguan wenti" 关于陶寺发掘报告编写及有关问题. In *Su Bingqi wenji* 苏秉琦文集 [Collected works of Su Bingqi], vol. 3. Beijing: Cultural Relics Press, 2009.

Taleb, Nassim Nicholas. *Antifragile: Things That Gain from Disorder*. New York: Random House, 2012.

Tang, Junyi 唐君毅. *Complete Works* 唐君毅全集. Taipei: Xuesheng shuju, 1991.

Tan, Qixiang 谭其骧. "Tangdai jimizhou shulun" 唐代羁縻州述论 [A discussion of loose-rein prefectures in the Tang dynasty]. In *Changshui cuibian* 长水粹编. Shijiazhuang: Hebei jiaoyu chubanshe, 2000.

Twitchett, Denis, and Michael Loewe. *The Cambridge History of China*, vol. 1: *The Ch'in and Han Empires 221 BC–AD 220*. Cambridge: Cambridge University Press, 1986.

Voegelin, Eric. *Order and History*, vol. 1: *Israel and Revelation*. Baton Rouge: Louisiana State University Press, 1956.

Wang, Fuzhi 王夫之. *Songlun* 宋论 [Commentary on the Song dynasty]. In *Complete Works* 船山全书, vol. 15. Changxia: Yuelu Publishing House, 1991.

Wang, Ke 王柯. *Minzu yu guojia: Zhongguo duo minzu tongyi guojia sixiang xipu* 民族与国家: 中国多民族统一国家思想系谱 [Nation and state: A genealogy of national state thought for the unification of China's many peoples]. Beijing: Chinese Academy of Social Sciences, 2001.

Wang, Mingming 王铭铭. "Zhongguo: Minzuti haishi wenmingti?" 中国: 民族体还是文明体? [China: A national body or a civilization body?]. *Wenhua zongheng* 文化纵横 12 (2008).

Wang, Tongling 王桐龄. *Zhongguo minzushi* 中国民族史 (A history of China's nationalities). Changchun: Jilin Publishing Group, 2010.

Wang, Wei 王巍. "Handai yiqian de sichou zhi lu" 汉代以前的丝绸之路 [The Silk Road in pre-Han times]. *Journal of the Chinese Academy of Social Sciences* 中国社会科学报 12 (January 2016).

Wittfogel, Karl A., and Feng Chia-sheng. *History of Chinese Society: Liao, 907–1125*. Philadelphia: American Philosophical Society, 1949.

Wittgenstein, Ludwig. *Philosophical Investigations*. London: Macmillan, 1964.

Xu, Hong 许宏. *Heyi Zhongguo* 何以中国 [Whence China?]. Beijing: SDX Joint Publishing, 2014.

———. *Zuizao de Zhongguo* 最早的中国 [The earliest China]. Beijing: Science Press, 2009.

Xu, Pingfang 徐萍芳. *Zhongguo chengshi kaoguxue lunji* 中国城市考古学论集 [Collected essays on the archaeology of Chinese towns]. Shanghai: Shanghai guji, 2015.

Xu, Zhongshu 徐中舒. *Guqiwu zhong de gudai wenhua zhidu* 古器物中的古代文化制度 [The ancient cultural institutions of ancient vessels]. Beijing: Commercial Press, 2015.

———, ed. *Jiaguwen zidian* 甲骨文字典 [Dictionary of the oracle bone script]. Chengdu: Sichuan Dictionary Press, 2014.

Yan, Mingshu 阎明恕. *Zhongguo gudai heqin shi* 中国古代和亲史 [A history of China's ancient dynastic marriage]. Guiyang: Guizhou Nationalities Press, 2003.

Yang, Boda 杨伯达. *Zhongguo yuqi quanji* 中国玉器全集 [Complete collection of Chinese jade artifacts], vol. 1. Shijiazhuang: Hebei Arts Press, 2005.

Yang, Kuan 杨宽. *Zhongguo gudai ducheng zhidu shi* 中国古代都城制度史 [A history of ancient China's urban organization]. Shanghai: Shanghai People's Press, 2006.

Yao, Dali 姚大力. *Meng-Yuan zhidu yu zhengzhi wenhua* 蒙元制度与政治文化 [The Mongolian Yuan dynasty organization and political culture]. Beijing: Peking University Press, 2011.

Yu, Lunian 俞鹿年. *Zhongguo zhengzhi zhidu tongshi* 中国政治制度通史第五卷 [A history of Chinese political institutions], vol. 5. Beijing: People's Press, 1996.

Yuan, Jing 袁靖. *Zhongguo dongwu kaoguxue* 中国动物考古学 [Chinese animal archaeology]. Beijing: Cultural Relics Press, 2015.

Zhang, Guangzhi 张光直. *Gudai Zhongguo kaoguxue* 古代中国考古学 [The archaeology of ancient China]. Beijing: SDX Joint Publishing, 2013. Chinese translation of *The Archaeology of China*, 4th edition. New Haven: Yale University Press, 1987.

———. *Kaoguxue zhuanti liu jiang* 考古学专题六讲 [Six lectures on archaeology]. Beijing: SDX Joint Publishing, 2013.

———. *Meishu: shenhua yu jisi* 美术: 神话与祭祀 [Aesthetics: Legends and rituals]. Beijing: SDX Joint Publishing, 2013. Chinese translation of *Art, Myth, and Ritual: The Path to Political Authority in Ancient China*. Cambridge, MA: Harvard University Press, 1983.

———. *Zhongguo kaoguxue lunwenji* 中国考古学论文集 [Anthology of articles on Chinese archaeology]. Beijing: SDX Joint Publishing, 1999.

Zhang, Wenjiang 张文江. *Shiji taishigong zixu jiangji* 史记太史公自序讲记 [Notes on the Grand Astrologer's authorial preface to *Records of the Historian*]. Shanghai: Shanghai wenyi Press, 2015.

Zhang, Xuecheng 章学诚. *Wenshi tongyi*, vol. 1: 文史通义 卷1: *Yijiao* A: 易教上 [The synoptic meaning of literature and history: Teachings on the *Changes* A]. Shanghai: Shanghai guji Press, 2008.

———. *Wenshi tongyi* 文史通义, 卷2: *Yuandao* A 原道上 [The synoptic meaning of literature and history, vol. 2: The original way part 1]. Shanghai: Shanghai guji Press, 2008.

Zhang, Zhaoyu 张兆裕. "*Mingdai hua-yi zhi bian*" 明代华夷之辨 [The distinction between the Chinese and the barbarians in the Ming dynasty]. In *Gushi wencun: Ming-Qing juanshang* 古史文存: 明清卷上 [Surviving ancient historical documents: Ming-Qing vol. 1], edited by the Institute of History, Chinese Academy of Social Sciences. Beijing: Social Sciences Documentation Press, 2004.

Zhao, Hui 赵辉. "*Yi zhongyuan wei zhongxin de lishi qushi de xingcheng*" 以中原为中心的历史趋势的形成 [The formation of the historical tendency that took the Central Plain as the center]. *Wenwu* 文物 1 (2000).

Zhao, Tingyang 赵汀阳. 天下的当代性: 世界秩序的实践与想象 [The contemporaneity of *tianxia*: Imagining and realizing a world order]. Beijing: Zhongxin Press, 2016.

———. *Diyi zhexue de zhidian* 第一哲学的支点 [The fulcrum of first philosophy]. Beijing: SDX Joint Publishing, 2013.

———. 天下体系: 世界制度哲学导论 [The *tianxia* system: An introduction to the philosophy of world institution]. Beijing: People's Press, 2011.

———. *Tianxia: tout sous un même ciel*. Paris: Éditions du Cerf, 2018.

Zheng, Youguo 郑有国. *Zhongguo shibo zhidu yanjiu* 中国市舶制度研究 [A study of China's maritime customs]. Fuzhou: Fujian Education Press, 2004.

Zhongguo shehui kexueyuan kaogu yanjiusuo 中国社会科学院考古研究所 [Archaeological Institute, Chinese Academy of Social Sciences]. *Zhongguo kaoguxue: Xia-Shang juan* 中国考古学: 夏商卷 [Chinese archaeology: Vol. Xia-Shang]. Beijing: Chinese Academy of Social Science Press, 2011.

———. *Zhongguo kaoguxue: xinshiqi shidai juan* 中国考古学: 新石器时代卷 [Chinese archaeology: Vol. Neolithic era]. Beijing: Chinese Academy of Social Science Press, 2010.

Zhou, Dingyang 周丁扬. *Tianxia de dangdaixing* 天下的当代性 [The contemporaneity of *tianxia*]. Beijing: Zhongxin Press, 2016.

Zhou, Zhenhe 周振鹤. *Zhongguo lishi zhengzhi dili 16 jiang* 中国历史政治地理十六讲 [16 lectures on Chinese historical-political geography]. Beijing: Zhonghua shuju, 2013.

Index

139

www.ingramcontent.com/pod-product-compliance
Lightning Source LLC
Chambersburg PA
CBHW030334270326
41926CB00010B/1628